Oxford AQA GCSE History (9-1)

Elizabethan England

c1568-1603

Revision Guide

 RECAP · APPLY · REVIEW · SUCCEED

Tim Williams

SERIES EDITOR
Aaron Wilkes

OXFORD

Great Clarendon Street, Oxford, OX2 6DP, United Kingdom

Oxford University Press is a department of the University of Oxford.

It furthers the University's objective of excellence in research, scholarship, and education by publishing worldwide. Oxford is a registered trade mark of Oxford University Press in the UK and in certain other countries.

British Library Cataloguing in Publication Data

Data available

978-0-19-842293-8

Kindle edition 978-0-19-842294-5

5 7 9 10 8 6

Paper used in the production of this book is a natural, recyclable product made from wood grown in sustainable forests.

The manufacturing process conforms to the environmental regulations of the country of origin.

Printed in Italy by L.E.G.O. S.p.A. - Lavis - TN

Acknowledgements

Cover: Dea Picture Library/Getty

Artworks: Aptara

The publisher would like to thank Jon Cloake for his work on the Student Book on which this Revision Guide is based, and Elisabeth Page for reviewing this Revision Guide.

We are grateful to the following for permission to include copyright material:

Express Newspapers/N & S Syndication for extract from 'All the Queen's Men: Was Elizabeth I really the Virgin Queen?' by Jane Warren, *Daily Express*, 4 July 2014, copyright © Express Newspapers 2014

Hartford Stage and the author for extract from 'Religion in Elizabethan England' by Aurelia Clunie

Immediate Media Company London Ltd for extract from 'Illegitimate Pretender', *History Extra*, 22 May 2015, copyright © BBC History/Immediate Media 2015

The MIT Press for extract from 'Poverty, Charity and Coercion in Elizabethan England' by Marjorie K McIntosh, The Journal of Interdisciplinary History, 35:3 (2005), pp 457-9, copyright © 2004 by the Massachussetts Institute of Technology and the editors of *The Journal of Interdisciplinary History*

We have made every effort to trace and contact all copyright holders before publication. If notified of any errors or omissions, the publisher will be happy to rectify these at the earliest opportunity.

Links to third party websites are provided by Oxford in good faith and for information only. Oxford disclaims any responsibility for the materials contained in any third party website referenced in this work.

From the author, Tim Williams: I would like to thank Aaron Wilkes, Becky DeLozier, Janice Chan, Tamsin Shelton, Sarah Jacobs and all at OUP for their hard work, support and guidance in the creation of this Revision Guide. Thanks must also go to Jon Cloake. Finally, thank you to my family, whose encouragement, support and love means so much.

Contents

Part one:
Elizabeth's court and Parliament

	RECAP	APPLY	REVIEW

Part two:
Life in Elizabethan times

RECAP   APPLY   REVIEW

Part three:
Troubles at home and abroad

Introduction

The *Oxford AQA GCSE History* textbook series has been developed by an expert team led by Jon Cloake and Aaron Wilkes. This matching revision guide offers you step-by-step strategies to master your AQA Depth Study: Elizabethan England exam skills, and the structured revision approach of **Recap, Apply and Review** to prepare you for exam success.

Use the **Checklists** on pages 3–4 to keep track of your revision, and use the traffic light feature on each page to monitor your confidence level on each topic. Other exam practice and revision features include **Top Revision Tips** on page 6, and the **'How to...'** guides for each exam question type on pages 7–9.

RECAP Each chapter recaps key events and developments through easy-to-digest chunks and visual diagrams. **Key terms** appear in bold and red; they are defined in the glossary. indicates the relevant Oxford AQA History Student Book pages so you can easily re-read the textbook for further revision.

SUMMARY highlights the most important facts at the end of each chapter.

TIMELINE provides a short list of dates to help you remember key events.

APPLY Each revision activity is designed to help drill your understanding of facts, and then progress towards applying your knowledge to exam questions.

These targeted revision activities are written specifically for this guide, which will help you apply your knowledge towards the four exam questions in your AQA Elizabethan England exam paper:

INTERPRETATION ANALYSIS   **EXPLAIN**   **WRITE AN ACCOUNT**   **HISTORIC ENVIRONMENT**

 Examiner Tip highlights key parts of an exam question, and gives you hints on how to avoid common mistakes in exams.

 Revision Skills provides different revision techniques. Research shows that using a variety of revision styles can help cement your revision.

 Review gives you helpful reminders about how to check your answers and how to revise further.

REVIEW Throughout each chapter, you can review and reflect on the work you have done, and find advice on how to further refresh your knowledge.

You can tick off the Review column from the progress checklist as you work through this revision guide. **Activity Answers Guidance** and the **Exam Practice** sections with full sample student answers also help you to review your own work.

Getting your revision right

It is perfectly natural to feel anxious when exam time approaches. The best way to keep on top of the stress is to be organised!

3 months to go

Plan: create a realistic revision timetable, and stick to it!

Track your progress: use the Progress Checklists (pages 3–4) to help you track your revision. It will help you stick to your revision plan.

Be realistic: revise in regular, small chunks, of around 30 minutes. Reward yourself with 10 minute breaks – you will be amazed how much more you'll remember.

Positive thinking: motivate yourself by turning your negative thoughts to positive ones. Instead of asking *'why can't I remember this topic at all?'* ask yourself *'what different techniques can I try to improve my memory?'*

Organise: make sure you have everything you need – your revision books, coloured pens, index cards, sticky notes, paper, etc. Find a quiet place where you are comfortable. Divide your notes into sections that are easy to use.

Timeline: create a timeline with colour-coded sticky notes, to make sure you remember important dates relating to the three parts of the Germany period study (use the Timeline on page 11 as a starting point).

Practise: ask your teachers for practice questions or past papers.

Revision techniques

Using a variety of revision techniques can help you remember information, so try out different methods:

- Make **flashcards**, using both sides of the card to test yourself on key figures, dates, and definitions
- **Colour-code** your notebooks
- **Reread** your textbook or copy out your notes
- Create **mind-maps** for complicated topics
- Draw **pictures** and symbols that spring to mind
- Group study
- Find a **buddy** or group to revise with and test you
- Listen to revision **podcasts** or watch revision **clips**
- Work through the **revision activities** in this guide.

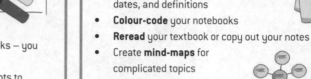

Revision tips to help you pass your Elizabethan England exam

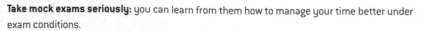

1 month to go

Key concepts: make sure you understand key concepts for this topic, such as patronage, succession, 'Golden Age' and excommunication. If you're unsure, attend revision sessions and ask your teacher.

Identify your weaknesses: which topics or question types are easier and which are more challenging for you? Schedule more time to revise the challenging topics or question types.

Make it stick: find memorable ways to remember chronology, using fun rhymes, or doodles, for example.

Take a break: do something completely different during breaks – listen to music, take a short walk, make a cup of tea, for example.

Check your answers: answer the exam questions in this guide, *then* check the Activity answers guidance at the end of the guide to practise applying your knowledge to exam questions.

Understand your mark scheme: review the Mark scheme (page 10) for each exam question, and make sure you understand how you will be marked.

Master your exam skills: study and remember the How to master your exam skills steps (pages 7–9) for each AQA question type – it will help you plan your answers quickly!

Time yourself: practise making plans and answering exam questions within the recommended time limits.

Take mock exams seriously: you can learn from them how to manage your time better under exam conditions.

Rest well: make sure your phone and laptop are put away at least an hour before bed. This will help you rest better.

On the big day

Sleep early: Don't work through the night, get a good night's sleep.

Be prepared: Make sure you know where and when the exam is, and leave plenty of time to get there.

Check: make sure you have all your equipment in advance, including spare pens!

Drink and eat healthily: avoid too much caffeine or junk food. Water is best – if you are 5% dehydrated, then your concentration drops 20%.

Stay focused: don't listen to people who might try to wind you up about what might come up in the exam – they don't know any more than you.

Good luck!

Master your exam skills

Get to grips with your Paper 2: Elizabethan England British Depth Study

The Paper 2 exam lasts 2 hours, and you have to answer eight questions covering two topics. The first four questions (worth 40 marks) will cover your Thematic Study topic; the last four questions (40 marks) will cover Elizabethan England. Here, you will find details about what to expect from the last four questions which relate to the British Depth Study topic Elizabethan England, and advice on how to master your exam skills.

You should spend about 50 minutes in total on the Elizabethan England questions – see pages 8–9 for how long to spend on each question.

The four questions will always follow this pattern:

▼ **INTERPRETATION C**

1   How convincing is **Interpretation A** about…? Explain your answer using **Interpretation A** and your contextual knowledge.

8 marks

2   Explain what was important about…

8 marks

3   Write an account of…

8 marks

4   How far does a study of… support this statement? Explain your answer. You should refer to… and your contextual knowledge.

16 marks

REVISION SKILLS

Read the *Thematic Study Revision Guide* for help on the first four questions of Paper 2.

EXAMINER TIP

For this question, you need to focus on the content of the interpretation and how it fits within your contextual knowledge.

EXAMINER TIP

You will already know what the historic environment site is for your exam. Make sure you are confident in explaining its features and how they relate to the historical context of Elizabethan England.

EXAMINER TIP

This question is worth a lot of marks and requires a longer answer. Make sure you leave plenty of time to complete it at the end of the exam.

REVIEW

If you find interpretations challenging, look out for the INTERPRETATION ANALYSIS activities throughout this guide to help you revise and drill your understanding of the 'interpretation' questions. Look out for the REVISION SKILLS ✓ tips too, to inspire you to find the revision strategies that work for you!

How to master the 'interpretation' question

Here are the steps to consider when answering the 'interpretation' question. Remember that this question is similar to the third 'interpretation' question in Paper 1, but this focuses on one interpretation only.

Question 1

- **Content:** Read through the interpretation carefully. What point is the writer making about the subject? Underline any key points or arguments that are made.

- **Context:** Now think back over your own knowledge. Does the content of the interpretation fit with what you know? Does it give a fair reflection of the person, event or issue it describes? Are its conclusions reasonable?

- **Conclude:** You now need to make a judgement about the interpretation. Do you find it convincing as an assessment of the person, event or issue it describes? Make sure you refer to the content of the interpretation and your own, relevant contextual knowledge in your answer.

- ⏱ Spend about 10 minutes on this 8-mark question.

How to master the 'explain' question

Here are the steps to consider when answering the 'explain' question. You may be asked to consider the importance of a key event/feature/person relating to cause and consequence ('why did it happen?' and 'what happened as a result?') or change and continuity ('what is different?' and 'what stayed the same?').

Question 2

- **Plan:** Think back over your knowledge of the topic referred to in the question to plan your answer. This question requires you to show strong knowledge and understanding of the event or issue stated.

- **Importance:** You need to say what made the event/feature/person *important*. In what ways did it have an impact on the wider historical period? Did it affect people's lives? Did it have an impact on politics or the government? Did it lead to change? What happened as a result?

- ⏱ Spend around 10 minutes on this 8-mark question.

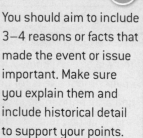

EXAMINER TIP

You should aim to include 3–4 reasons or facts that made the event or issue important. Make sure you explain them and include historical detail to support your points.

How to master the 'write an account' question

Here are the steps to consider when answering the 'write an account' question. This question involves telling the key moments of an event in relation to the topic of the question. You need to describe, explain and analyse how one development led to another.

Question 3

- **Select the key moments:** What will you include in your story? Spend 1 minute to work out 3–4 key moments that are *relevant* to the question. Make sure you organise the moments in chronological order (starting with the earliest). You must include 1–2 specific historical facts for each key moment and plenty of specific historical detail.

- **Link your story:** Write your answer based on the key moments you have identified, and explain *how* the moments link together to cause the event to develop. Make sure you link your answer to the point of the question. A top-level answer will also include an explanation of the consequences of the events on the wider historical period of Elizabethan England.

- ⏱ You should spend about 10 minutes on this 8-mark question.

EXAMINER TIP

Use phrases like 'this led to …' and 'as a result of this …' to help you to structure your answer.

How to master the 'historic environment' question

The last question in Paper 2 will always relate to the historic environment. You have to show how your knowledge of the specific site helps you to understand the key features of Elizabethan England. In other words, what can a study of the historic environment tell you about people or events at the time?

Question 4

- **Read the question carefully:** What statement is the question asking you to consider? The statement is located within the quotation marks. Underline key words in the statement to help you focus your answer.

- **Plan your essay:** Consider the questions below.

  o **Motivation:** Why was the site created?

  o **Location:** Why is it in this particular location?

  o **Function:** Why was it built in this specific way? Identify and explain specific building features, and the job they do.

  o **Purpose:** What was the building used for? Who lived or worked there? How is its purpose reflected in the design?

- If the site is a battle (such as the defeat of the Spanish Armada), you should consider instead: Why was the battle fought (**motivation**)? Why was it fought in that particular **location**? What happened at the battle?

- **Context:** Now that you have considered your specific historic site, you need to consider what it tells you about the Elizabethan period. The question will guide you in this. You need to select *relevant* information about the motivation/location/function/purpose which reflects the aspect of the Elizabethan era mentioned in the exam question (you should have underlined this aspect). Your answer needs to link your knowledge of the period with your knowledge of the site.

- **Conclude:** This question will ask you 'how far …' the historic site has helped you to back up a statement about Elizabethan England, so make sure you come to a clear conclusion when you answer this question.

- ⏱ You should spend around 20 minutes on this 16-mark question.

REVIEW

You can find sample student answers to each question type in the Exam Practice pages at the end of this guide.

EXAMINER TIP

Don't forget you will also have to answer four questions relating to your Thematic Study in Paper 2. Ensure you leave enough time to complete both sections of Paper 2! You are advised to spend 50 minutes on your Thematic Study in the exam.

AQA GCSE History mark schemes

Below are simplified versions of the AQA mark schemes, to help you understand the marking criteria for your **Paper 2: Elizabethan England** exam.

Level	'Interpretation' question
4	• Complex evaluation of the interpretation. • Argument about how convincing the interpretation is, is shown throughout the answer, supported by relevant facts/understanding. 7–8 marks
3	• Developed evaluation of the interpretation referring to at least two aspects of the interpretation. • Argument is stated about how convincing the interpretation is. Answer is supported by relevant facts/understanding. 5–6 marks
2	• Simple answer referring to one aspect of the interpretation. • Answer is supported with relevant facts/understanding. 3–4 marks
1	• Basic answer on the interpretation. • Some facts/understanding are shown. 1–2 marks

Level	'Explain' question
4	• Complex explanation of several consequences/causes/changes. • A range of accurate, detailed and relevant facts are shown. 7–8 marks
3	• Developed explanation of two or more consequences/causes/changes. • A range of accurate, relevant facts are shown. 5–6 marks
2	• Simple explanation of one consequence/cause/change. • Specific relevant facts are shown. 3–4 marks
1	• Basic explanation of consequences/causes/changes. • Some basic related facts are shown. 1–2 marks

Level	'Write an account' question
4	• Complex analysis of consequences/causes/changes. • A carefully selected story with a range of accurate and relevant facts is shown. 7–8 marks
3	• Developed analysis of consequence/cause/change. • Structured and well-ordered story with a range of accurate and relevant facts is shown. 5–6 marks
2	• Simple analysis of consequence/cause/change. • Structured story with specific relevant facts is shown. 3–4 marks
1	• Basic analysis of consequence/cause/change. • Straightforward story with some basic related facts is shown. 1–2 marks

Level	'Historic environment' question
4	• Complex explanation of consequences/causes/changes. • Argument is shown throughout the structured answer, supported by a range of accurate, detailed and relevant facts about the site and the wider historical period. 13–16 marks
3	• Developed explanation of changes. • Argument is shown throughout the structured answer, supported by a range of accurate and relevant facts about the site. 9–12 marks
2	• Simple explanation of changes. • Argument is shown, supported by specific, relevant facts about the site. 5–8 marks
1	• Basic explanation of changes. • Some basic related facts about the site are shown. 1–4 marks

Elizabethan England c1568–1603 Timeline

The colours represent different types of event as follows:

Blue: economic events   Red: political events

Black: international events or foreign policies   Yellow: social events

Green: plots and rebellions

1558 — **November** – Elizabeth crowned Queen of England at the age of 25

1559 — Elizabeth's religious settlement

1569 — **November** – The Northern Rebellion

1570 — Norwich authorities conducted first survey of the poor, model for Poor Law of 1601

1570 — **April** – The Pope issues the *Regnans in Excelsis*, which excommunicates Elizabeth from the Catholic Church

1571 — **November** – The Ridolfi Plot

1580 — Jesuit priests begin to arrive in England from Europe

1580 — **September** – Sir Francis Drake completes the first circumnavigation of the globe

1585 — Elizabeth sends troops to the Netherlands to support Dutch Protestant rebels

1583 — John Whitgift appointed Archbishop of Canterbury and cracks down on Puritanism

1586 — **July** – The Babington Plot is discovered, leading to the trial of Mary, Queen of Scots

1587 — Roanoke colony is established in North America

February – Mary, Queen of Scots is executed

1588 — **July–September** – The Spanish Armada

1590 — First of several bad harvests leads to food shortages; many country people begin to move to the towns

1599 — Opening of the Globe Theatre in London

1600 — Establishment of the East India Company

1601 — **February** – Essex's rebellion

Poor Law introduced

1603 — **March** – Elizabeth I dies and is succeeded by James I

CHAPTER 1 — Elizabeth and her court

Queen Elizabeth I, reigned 1558–1603

When she was born, no one ever expected Elizabeth to become monarch. Her mother, **Anne Boleyn**, had been executed for treason on the orders of her father, King **Henry VIII**. Further, Elizabeth's elder sister, Queen **Mary I of England**, saw her as a potential threat to her own rule. The family tree shows how unlikely Elizabeth's coronation would have seemed when she was a child. She was the middle of Henry's three children and both her younger brother and her older sister came before her in the line of succession. Yet, as a princess, Elizabeth had been educated and brought up within the royal household. She learned quickly that the court could be a dangerous place for her if she was not careful in what she said, did, and whom she trusted.

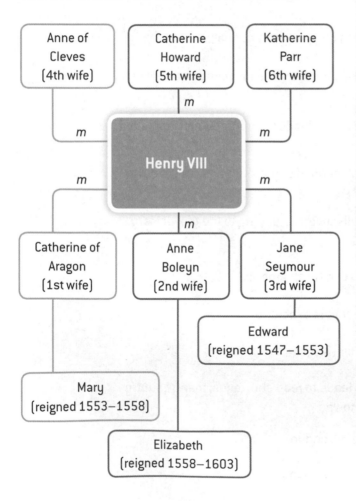

Power in Elizabethan England

Elizabeth was only 25 when she became queen and she needed to establish her authority quickly. Although being queen gave her power, she could not do as she pleased. Her government had a clear structure of advisors and other powerful figures. Most of the power was held by a few key trusted individuals in Elizabeth's court. Many, but not all, of these were **privy councillors**. The queen could ensure support through **patronage**.

Patronage was an important way of ensuring loyalty from courtiers. Elizabeth could award titles, land, monopolies and other powerful positions and money-making opportunities in exchange for obedience and support.

Court life

The **royal court** and the government were not the same thing. The court was made up of all the officials, servants and advisors that surrounded Elizabeth. The court was the centre of power, but also the source of the latest trends and fashions. It included the Privy Council, but Justices of the Peace and Parliament were not part of it. The government was made up of the queen and her closest advisors, usually privy councillors, but always men whom she trusted.

Lord Lieutenants

- Appointed by the queen.
- Responsible for running a particular area of the country.
- Responsible for raising a militia to fight for the queen if needed.
- Many also served on the Privy Council.

Parliament

- Made up of the House of Lords and the House of Commons.
- Had influence over tax and was responsible for passing laws.
- The queen could choose when to call Parliament and was free to ignore their advice.

Who had power?

Privy Council

- Responsible for the day-to-day running of the country, dealing with all policy areas.
- Although the queen could technically appoint whoever she wished, in reality she had to appoint the most powerful landowners in the country, in order to prevent rebellion.
- If the council was united, it was almost impossible for Elizabeth to go against their wishes. However, unity was very rare in a group filled with ambitious rivals.
- Led by the **Secretary of State**.
- William Cecil and Francis Walsingham were two significant and powerful figures who each served as Secretary of State. Both had a huge influence on Elizabeth.

Justices of the Peace

- Several in every county.
- Responsible for maintaining order and enforcing the law.

SUMMARY

- When Elizabeth was a child, no one expected her to be queen.
- The most powerful group in Elizabethan England was the Privy Council, led by the Secretary of State. It was responsible for the daily running of the country.
- Parliament had influence over tax and passing laws, but its power was limited.
- Lord Lieutenants were appointed by the queen to run a particular area of the country.
- The royal court was the centre of Elizabethan power and the source of the latest trends and fashions.

APPLY

EXPLAIN

a List as many reasons as you can why someone might be appointed to a position of power in Elizabethan England.

b Write a few sentences to explain the role of the Privy Council in governing the country during Elizabeth's reign.

EXAMINER TIP

These steps are good preparation for answering an 'explain' question on the importance of the Privy Council.

WRITE AN ACCOUNT

 EXAM QUESTION Write an account of how Elizabethan government worked.

The difficulties of a female ruler

RECAP

The problems Elizabeth faced

When Elizabeth came to the throne in 1558, aged 25, she immediately had a number of problems to deal with. She was a young woman in a country where men had always held the power.

Succession

- Elizabeth was the last living child of Henry VIII and she had no children of her own. So it was unclear who would **succeed** her if she died before producing an heir. In the past, situations like this had led to violent struggles for power.
- In 1562, she nearly died of smallpox. This drew attention to the uncertainty of England's future. As a result, senior figures were keen that she marry as soon as possible.

REVIEW

If you are unsure about the religious differences that existed at the time, have a look at pages 36–45 to remind yourself of these.

Religion

- The Tudor period had seen England's official religion change a number of times, and this had created instability and violence.
- Many Catholics did not trust Elizabeth and some claimed that she had no right to be queen (they did not recognise Henry's marriage to Elizabeth's mother).
- Puritanism, an extreme form of Protestantism, was also seen as a threat. There were a number of Puritans who had hoped to take control of Elizabeth's Church and make it more extreme – this could have damaged the whole religious settlement.

Foreign policy

- Catholic countries like Spain and France wanted influence over England and had the support of the Pope in this aim. The threat of invasion was very real.
- One key area of tension was the Netherlands, where the Protestant population was in conflict with its Spanish rulers. Elizabeth had to decide whether or not to become involved.

Elizabeth's problems

Taxation

- The country was short of money and Elizabeth needed to raise taxes.
- Poverty was widespread and raising taxes would be very unpopular.

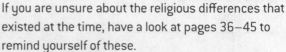

Mary, Queen of Scots

- With no direct heir, the next in line to the throne was Elizabeth's Catholic cousin, Mary. Many Catholics saw her as an alternative Queen of England and this made her a serious threat to Elizabeth.

REVIEW

The diagram gives a brief summary of the problems that Elizabeth faced. All of them are dealt with in more detail in the following chapters.

Ireland

- Like her predecessors, Elizabeth considered herself to be Queen of Ireland. In 1559, she faced a major revolt in Ireland – the first of several during her reign.

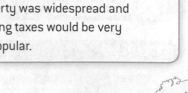

 **APPLY**

REVISION SKILLS

A mind-map is a useful way to revise this topic. Copy the mind-map below. Identify links between the individual problems and add these to your diagram making sure you explain them. For example, how does the challenge of religion link to Mary, Queen of Scots?

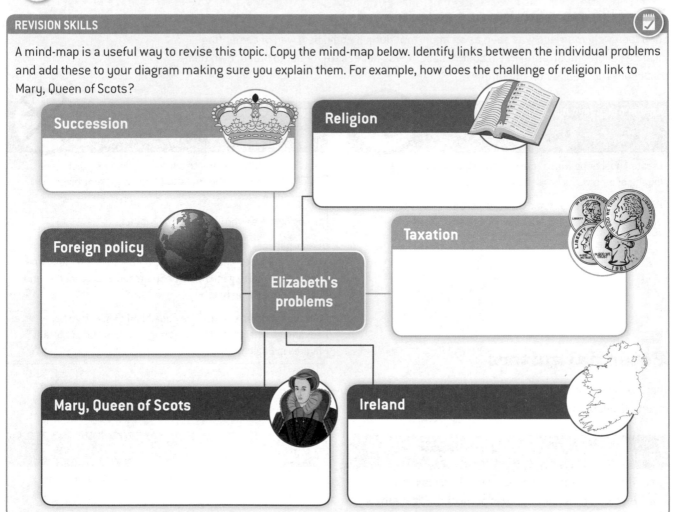

EXPLAIN

a Complete the table below to explain why each problem was such a concern for Elizabeth.

Problem	Why was it such a concern for Elizabeth?
Succession	
Religion	
Foreign policy	
Taxation	
Ireland	
Mary, Queen of Scots	

b **EXAM QUESTION** Explain what was important about the problems that Elizabeth faced at the beginning of her reign.

EXAMINER TIP

For an 'explain' question, make sure you say *why* each issue caused a problem for Elizabeth — don't just describe it.

Marriage and succession

For a monarch, marriage was seen as an important duty. It could be a way of cementing alliances. More importantly in Elizabeth's case, it was necessary for her to produce an heir that could succeed her on the throne.

Arguments in favour of marriage	Arguments against marriage
Create an alliance with a foreign country or guarantee the loyalty of a powerful English family.	Loss of authority – either to a foreign ruler or Englishman. By not marrying, Elizabeth – and England – kept their independence.
Produce an heir to continue the Tudor line and stop Mary, Queen of Scots from becoming queen when Elizabeth died.	Giving birth was very risky for the mother.
	Her experience of marriage had been bad – her father had married six times and ordered her mother to be executed and her sister's marriage to Philip of Spain had been unhappy and did not produce an heir.
	Elizabeth was able to use the possibility of marriage to her advantage when dealing with foreign leaders and important figures in England.

Potential suitors

There was no shortage of men who were ready to marry the queen. Three of the most important are shown here.

Francis, Duke of Anjou and Alençon

- The French King's brother and heir to his throne.
- By the time a marriage was proposed, Elizabeth was 46 and probably beyond having children. A childless marriage could result in England falling under French control.
- He was Catholic and many important figures in Elizabeth's court were against the marriage.

King Philip II of Spain

- One of the wealthiest and most powerful men in the world.
- He had been married to Elizabeth's sister, Queen Mary I, but he had rarely visited England and the marriage had not produced an heir.
- He was Catholic.

Robert Dudley, Earl of Leicester

- A childhood friend of the queen and a favourite of hers throughout her reign. Many assumed they were in love.
- A key figure in the royal court and a member of the Privy Council.
- When his wife died, he became free to marry Elizabeth but the scandal surrounding her death (and rumours of his involvement) meant this was almost impossible.

Why didn't Elizabeth get married?

We will never know for sure why Elizabeth chose to remain unmarried. Elizabeth herself said that she was married to 'the kingdom of England' and that remaining single allowed her to focus totally on ruling her country and keep England secure and independent.

 **APPLY**

EXPLAIN

a Why were people so keen for Elizabeth to marry?

_____

_____

_____

b Give three reasons why Elizabeth's decision not to marry might be considered a clever one.

_____

_____

_____

c **EXAM QUESTION** Explain what was important about the issue of Elizabeth's marriage.

EXAMINER TIP

For this question, you need to include arguments both for and against Elizabeth's marriage to show why it was such an important issue.

INTERPRETATION ANALYSIS

a Look at this interpretation about Elizabeth's view on marriage:

▼ **INTERPRETATION A** *From a newspaper interview with Alison Weir, who wrote a novel based on Queen Elizabeth's life:*

> Although Elizabeth loved Dudley she certainly did not want to marry him, or any other man. The reason goes back to a childhood that would have been considered highly dysfunctional in modern terms. Elizabeth hated the idea of marriage. This is understandable when you consider that her father was Henry VIII and her mother was his second wife, Anne Boleyn whom her father ordered beheaded when Elizabeth was just three. Her stepmothers didn't fare so well either. At the age of eight she declared she would never marry.

b The priority when reading an interpretation is to decide what point it is making. What reason does the interpretation suggest for Elizabeth's decision not to marry?

c **EXAM QUESTION** How convincing is **Interpretation A** about Elizabeth's decision not to marry? Explain your answer using the interpretation and your own knowledge.

REVIEW

If you are unsure about how to analyse the interpretation, review the step-by-step guide on page 8 about how to master your interpretation analysis exam skills.

Relations with Parliament

By far the most challenging relationship that Elizabeth had was the one with Parliament. All the key issues of her reign were debated in Parliament and it was vital that she had its support.

What was Parliament?

- Consisted of lords, bishops and other nobles who sat in the House of Lords and 'commoners' (Members of Parliament – MPs) who sat in the House of Commons.
- Its role was to discuss issues and advise the queen.
- Responsible for passing laws and setting taxes.
- Although the queen could decide when to call Parliament (allow it to meet) and did not have to listen to what it said, in practice she could not ignore it completely. She needed to deal with Parliament very carefully.

Marriage and succession

Many in Parliament saw it as their duty to find Elizabeth a suitable husband and, by 1566, began to discuss the issue openly. Angry at such interference, she banned them from talking about it again. Elizabeth saw marriage as a decision for her alone.

Religion

The most divisive factor in Elizabethan society was religion and Parliament reflected this. The majority of those in both houses of Parliament were Protestants and supported Elizabeth's religious settlement. When Elizabeth wished to introduce laws that made life hard for Catholics, she found support in Parliament. One area of disagreement, however, was over the issue of Puritanism. A number of powerful Puritans in Parliament tried unsuccessfully to introduce new laws to change the Church of England.

Freedom of speech

An MP named Peter Wentworth was arrested three times during Elizabeth's reign for arguing that MPs should be allowed to speak on any matter they chose. Elizabeth clearly did not agree! Some MPs supported Wentworth's view, but others did not. One of his arrests was organised by other MPs wishing to demonstrate their loyalty to Elizabeth.

Parliament under Elizabeth I

Crime and poverty

The issue of poverty was significant in Elizabethan England, particularly when it led to crime. Many MPs recognised that simply punishing the poor did not work and attempted to introduce new poor laws. They were unsuccessful, until 1601, when the Poor Law was finally passed.

Mary, Queen of Scots

The majority of those in Parliament saw Mary, a Catholic, as a clear threat to national security and a significant number of them called for her execution. This pressure, and that of the Privy Council, may have swayed the hesitant Elizabeth into executing her cousin.

Monopolies

The giving of **monopolies** was an important way for Elizabeth to maintain the loyalty of powerful men in England (for example, the sweet wine monopoly given to the Earl of Essex). In 1571, an MP named Robert Bell criticised them as unfair. Other MPs joined him in calling for changes in their use. Elizabeth agreed to make a few changes but MPs pushed for more. In 1601, she made a speech to Parliament in which she cleverly managed to give the impression that she was agreeing to make major changes to how monopolies worked without actually promising very much at all.

Revision cards would be a useful way of revising Parliament under Elizabeth. Create a set of cards using the spider diagram on the previous page. On one side write the headings of each branch (for example, Mary, Queen of Scots) and on the other, briefly outline Parliament's response to the issue.

How did Elizabeth manage Parliament?

- She made it clear that she was in charge through her words and actions, issuing regular statements about her authority and arresting MPs who went too far in criticising her.
- She had the ability to dismiss Parliament when she wished and could also appoint new members to the House of Lords.
- It was the duty of her privy councillors and nobles to manage Parliament and ensure that they were clear on her wishes.

 **APPLY**

EXPLAIN

a Copy and complete the table.

Difficulties between Elizabeth and Parliament	Examples of when the relationship was good

b Explain what was important about Parliament during Elizabeth's reign.

EXAMINER TIP

Remember that in an 'explain' question you should aim to go beyond describing what Parliament is. Include specific details about its role.

WRITE AN ACCOUNT

a What was Parliament's role in Elizabethan England?

b Produce an A3 learning poster about Parliament under Elizabeth. Use the spider diagram on page 18 to help you. Creating large learning posters on key topics helps you to gain an overview in preparation for the 'write an account' questions.

c Write an account of Elizabeth I's relationship with her Parliament.

EXAMINER TIP

For a 'write an account' question, you must include specific detail, including key events and dates from Elizabeth's reign.

REVIEW

Parliament was a key part of how England was governed during Elizabeth's reign. Look back at Chapter 1 to remind yourself where it fits in the structure of Elizabethan government.

The strength of Elizabeth's authority and Essex's rebellion

REVIEW

To revise the rebellions Elizabeth faced, turn to page 44.

Elizabeth faced a number of rebellions and challenges to her authority during her reign. Most were connected to religion. The final challenge, though, was all about power and influence. In 1601, the Earl of Essex led a rebellion against his queen.

Background

- Essex had been a loyal subject throughout Elizabeth's reign and was, for a time, one of her favourites. He became a privy councillor in 1595 and was awarded the monopoly on sweet wine in England.
- During his time at court, Essex developed a rivalry with Robert Cecil, the son of the powerful William Cecil and an important and influential figure at court.
- Essex pleased the queen when, in 1596, he successfully attacked the Spanish port of Cadiz.

Causes of the rebellion

- Soon after his victory against the Spanish, Essex became involved in an argument with the queen during a Privy Council meeting. At one point, he turned his back on Elizabeth and she hit him on the side of the head. He nearly drew his sword but was stopped by other councillors just in time. Essex was placed under house arrest.
- Later the queen sent him to Ireland to deal with a rebellion. He not only failed to defeat the rebels but agreed a truce with them – directly against the queen's orders.
- On his return to England, Essex rushed straight into the queen's chambers and caught her without her wig!
- After his failures in Ireland, Essex quickly fell from Elizabeth's favour. She refused to renew his sweet wine monopoly. As a result, he lost much of his wealth and influence.
- Angry, and with nothing left to lose, Essex began to gather supporters and plot a rebellion against the queen.

The rebellion

- In February 1601, Essex took four privy councillors hostage and marched them to his London house, along with 200 supporters.
- Robert Cecil, Essex's great rival, responded by labelling him a traitor. Many of Essex's supporters left, while others panicked and released the hostages without his permission.
- Essex and his remaining followers were arrested.

Consequences

- Essex was put on trial for treason and was sentenced to death.
- During his interrogation, he agreed to name other rebels including his sister, Penelope.
- He was executed in private on 25 February 1601. Some of his supporters were also put to death but most were just fined.
- Elizabeth had made it clear, even late in her reign, that she would not tolerate challenges to her authority.

SUMMARY

What challenges did Elizabeth face during her reign?

- She was a female ruler in a time when women did not hold positions of authority.

- She had a number of initial problems to deal with, including religion, foreign policy, taxation, Ireland, Mary, Queen of Scots, and succession.

- Elizabeth never married despite many suitors. Some saw this as a clever decision.

- Elizabeth had to deal with Parliament, and a number of disagreements and tensions arose – particularly around religion, monopolies and Mary, Queen of Scots.

- Essex's rebellion was the final challenge to Elizabeth's authority and it was easily defeated.

 **APPLY**

EXPLAIN

a Create a set of revision cards showing the causes of Essex's rebellion. You could use the following headings:

- Argument with Elizabeth
- Failures in Ireland
- Loss of monopoly and wealth

b Now rank them in order of importance. You must be able to justify your decisions.

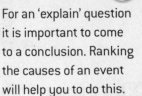

EXAMINER TIP

For an 'explain' question it is important to come to a conclusion. Ranking the causes of an event will help you to do this.

WRITE AN ACCOUNT

a Create a spider diagram showing the causes of Essex's rebellion.

b Create a flow chart showing the events of the rebellion.

c **EXAM QUESTION** Write an account of the failure of the Earl of Essex's rebellion.

EXAMINER TIP

Remember, for a 'write an account' question you need to explain what made the rebellion such an important event and what its failure tells us about Elizabeth's authority.

CHAPTER 3

A 'Golden Age'

📖 RECAP

Elizabethan society was highly structured and everyone knew their place within it. Here is a very simplified version of the 'Great Chain of Being'.

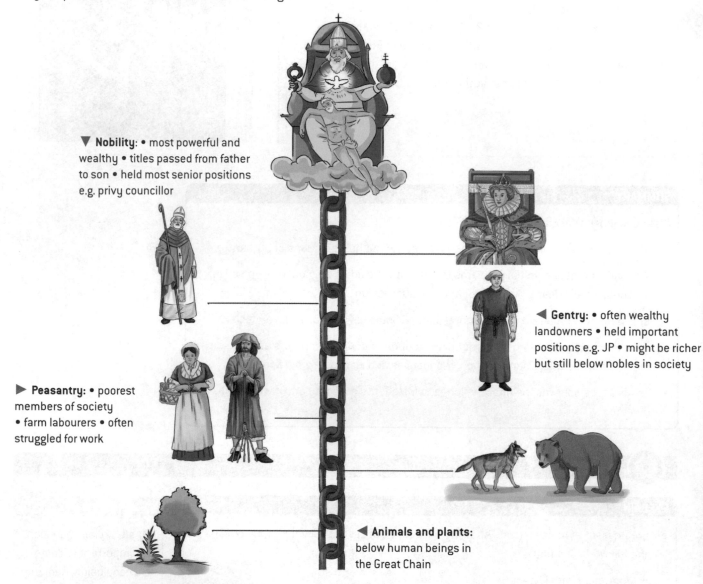

▼ **Nobility**: • most powerful and wealthy • titles passed from father to son • held most senior positions e.g. privy councillor

◀ **Gentry**: • often wealthy landowners • held important positions e.g. JP • might be richer but still below nobles in society

▶ **Peasantry**: • poorest members of society • farm labourers • often struggled for work

◀ **Animals and plants**: below human beings in the Great Chain

The rise of the gentry

Before Elizabeth's reign, almost all wealth was held by the nobility. The stability that the Elizabethan period brought began to change this. People could make money from trade. The gentry grew as a result and began to fill powerful positions by becoming members of Parliament and Justices of the Peace.

Hardwick Hall

Bess of Hardwick, also known as Elizabeth Shrewsbury, built Hardwick Hall between 1590 and 1597. It was one of the grandest houses in Elizabethan England and a way to demonstrate her wealth and position in society.

Changing homes of the gentry

One way in which the gentry and the nobility could show off their wealth and privilege was by building lavish country homes:

- Purpose: no longer defence, but to display **refined taste.**

- Usually **symmetrical** with open courtyards, unlike the closed, secure ones that went before.

- Lots of **expensive glass** windows showed owner's wealth.

- Medieval great hall replaced by a **great chamber**.

- **Privacy**: number of rooms increased, separating servants from owners.

Decorative stonework reflected fashionable Italian design. 'ES' stands for Elizabeth Shrewsbury and her coat of arms is at the front of the house.

Straight chimney columns placed within the internal walls, to be symmetrical and reflect classical design.

Elaborate geometric plasterwork reflected the latest **Renaissance** fashions.

Great chamber for entertaining guests; included several portraits of the queen.

Large glass windows with lattice frames

Portraits showed family connections. Oak wall panelling told classical stories, and kept heat in. The carved overmantel above the fireplace references the Hardwick and Cavendish families.

Long gallery for entertaining guests and winter exercise. Two massive chimney pieces contain statues of Justice and Mercy.

Loggia inspired by Italian Renaissance architecture.

Hardwick Hall: details of the interior and exterior

⚙ APPLY

EXPLAIN

a Create your own version of the 'Great Chain of Being', adding details about the role of the three classes (nobility, gentry and peasantry).

b **EXAM QUESTION** Explain what was important about the 'Great Chain of Being' in Elizabethan society.

EXAMINER TIP
You need to explain how the 'Great Chain of Being' acted as a guide to the structure of Elizabethan society.

HISTORIC ENVIRONMENT

a Create a table. In the first column, write down the features of Hardwick Hall. In the second, explain how each one demonstrated the wealth and success of Bess of Hardwick.

b **EXAM QUESTION** 'The main reason for building a stately home in Elizabethan times was to demonstrate the success and wealth of its owner.' How far does a study of Hardwick Hall support this statement? Explain your answer. You should refer to Hardwick Hall and your contextual knowledge.

EXAMINER TIP
Include specific references to the historic environment mentioned and demonstrate your wider knowledge of the period.

The theatre in Elizabethan England

Writers, actors and theatre troupes

- Playwrights like William Shakespeare produced new works every year. These included comedies, histories and tragedies.

- Acting was an entirely male profession, with female roles played by boys.

- Popular actors like Richard Burbage became very famous and would often return to roles many times or have parts written specifically for them.

- Works were performed by theatre **troupes** such as the Lord Chamberlain's Men (of which both Shakespeare and Burbage were members). Companies were named after the people who provided their funding: the **patron**. Being a patron was a good way to impress the queen, who was very fond of the theatre.

The theatre

The Elizabethan period saw a major change in how theatre worked, with the building of the first permanent theatres. Both rich and poor now attended performances, whereas previously theatre had been seen as something for ordinary people, usually performed in the back room of an inn.

The galleries: seated, covered areas for the rich

Roof: over the stage, often called the 'heavens'. Ropes and rigging were used for scene changes and dramatic entrances

Lords' rooms: most expensive seats; sometimes used by actors and musicians during performances (often called a Juliet balcony)

Gentlemen's rooms: balconies on either side, seats at around 4 pence

Tiring room: room where the actors put on their attire

Stage: often decorated with scenery and almost always a trapdoor for special effects like smoke; back wall was called the Frons Scenae and had a door for actors to enter and exit

Pit: where ordinary people stood to watch, often heckling the actors; completely open to the weather

The Globe Theatre in London, built in 1599

- Despite scientific breakthroughs in some areas, other practices were questionable – alchemy (turning cheap metal into gold) and astrology (using the planets to predict the future) were very popular.

The idea of a 'golden age' was encouraged by Elizabeth and her government. Plays, festivals and pamphlets (small booklets) promoted the idea. The term **Gloriana** was used to describe the spreading of this message. For Elizabeth, this was a useful way of securing her popularity and her throne.

SUMMARY

- Elizabethan society had a very rigid structure with the monarch at the top, followed by the nobles, the gentry and then the peasantry.

- One important way of demonstrating wealth and success was through the building of grand country houses.

- The theatre was an important part of life for many Elizabethans. Rich and poor came together to watch plays.

- The Elizabethan era was seen as a 'golden age' because of the many accomplishments, but some question whether this is an accurate description.

 APPLY

INTERPRETATION ANALYSIS

a Was Elizabeth's reign a 'golden age' for England? Complete the table below using information from these two pages to help you answer the question.

Yes	No

REVIEW

You will need to use your knowledge from across the period for this question. In particular, look back at the previous pages of this chapter and at pages 32–35.

b Look at this interpretation about an Elizabethan 'Golden Age':

▼ **INTERPRETATION A** *Adapted from an article by Aurelia Clunie on the Hartford Stage theatre website*:

> Queen Elizabeth I was an incredibly popular queen whose reign is remembered as a 'golden age' of culture and growth. The Elizabethan Era is known for Sir Francis Drake's exploration of the 'new world,' the English defeat of the Spanish Armada and Sir Walter Raleigh's colonial exploration, the development of the Shakespearean theatre and the beginnings of an English overseas empire. Yet it was also a time marked by war, economic depression, and religious conflict. Deep tensions between Protestants and Catholics came from England's recent break with the Roman Catholic Church by Elizabeth's father, Henry VIII.

- What point is the interpretation making about the Elizabethan era?

c

EXAM QUESTION How convincing is **Interpretation A** about the Elizabethan 'Golden Age'? Explain your answer using the interpretation and your contextual knowledge.

EXAMINER TIP

You need to be clear about what point the interpretation is making and then use your own knowledge to bring in other arguments. This will allow you to judge how far you find the interpretation convincing.

WRITE AN ACCOUNT

a Explain what is meant by 'Gloriana'.

b

EXAM QUESTION Write an account of the ways in which the idea of a 'golden age' could be seen as a myth created by Elizabeth.

EXAMINER TIP

Explain how and why the period could be described as a 'golden age'. Do not just describe its key features.

CHAPTER 4 — The poor

RECAP

At the bottom of Elizabethan society were the ordinary people. For many, life was straight forward: they worked for their lord and could provide for themselves and their families. For those without this security, life could be very difficult. Those without work were known as **paupers**. Paupers relied on charity to survive. This meant begging or going to the local church for help.

Poverty in Elizabethan England rose significantly for a number of reasons:

Actions of previous monarchs

- Henry VII limited the right of nobles to hold private armies, fearing they might be a threat to his throne. This left many soldiers without work.
- The Reformation under Henry VIII led to the closure of the monasteries. Monks, nuns and other Church employees were left with nowhere to live or work.
- The closure of the monasteries also left the sick and poor with no one to care for them.
- Economic problems under Henry VIII and Edward VI led to the collapse of the cloth trade and the loss of many jobs.

Changes in agriculture

- Bad harvests between 1594 and 1598 led to food shortages and starvation in parts of England. The food shortage also increased prices – which led to **inflation**.
- Increasing numbers of landlords began to keep sheep on their land rather than grow crops. This system, known as **enclosure**, meant that fewer workers were needed.
- Many unemployed farm workers headed to towns and cities in search of employment. There were not enough jobs to go around.

Reasons for poverty in Elizabethan England

Population increase

- During Elizabeth's reign, England's population went from 2.8 million to 4 million.
- A shortage of places to live gave power to landlords who increased rents (**rack renting**).

Flu outbreak

- A terrible outbreak of flu in 1556 killed 200,000 people, including many farm workers.

Attitudes and responses to poverty

The deserving poor

- The 'Great Chain of Being' made it clear to many nobles that they were simply 'better' than the poor.
- Many believed it was their duty to help those below them in society.
- They recognised that many paupers could not help their situation and were not to blame for their poverty.
- Charities for the poor grew and **almshouses** were established.

REVIEW

Look back at page 22 to remind yourself about the 'Great Chain of Being'.

The undeserving poor

- Some paupers were seen as undeserving: untrustworthy beggars who had no interest in honest work.

- *Warning Against Vagabonds* by Thomas Harman, published in 1567, encouraged the view that many poor people were merely confidence tricksters or criminals. Others were seen as being idle or lazy.

The vagabonds described by Harman included many scammers and confidence tricksters:

- The Counterfeit Crank bit soap so that he frothed at the mouth. People would feel sympathy and give him money.
- Baretop Trickster women would trick men into following them by removing clothing. The men would then be beaten and robbed by her accomplices.
- The Clapper Dudgeon would cut himself and tie dirty bandages around the wounds to gain sympathy.
- Tom O'Bedlam would pretend to be mad. He might stick a chicken's head in his ear or bark like a dog.

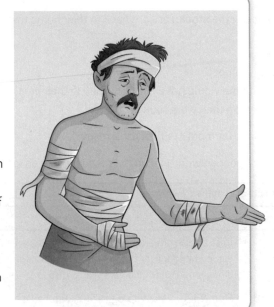

 APPLY

EXPLAIN

a What is meant by the term 'undeserving poor'?

_____

_____

_____

b Create a mind-map on attitudes to poverty in Elizabethan England. Include references to both the deserving and undeserving poor.

WRITE AN ACCOUNT

a Make a list of the reasons for poverty in Elizabethan England.

b **EXAM QUESTION** Write an account of how poverty became widespread in Elizabethan England.

 EXAMINER TIP

For this type of question make sure you explain the reasons that led to the increase in poverty, as well as describing what happened. Try to make links between the reasons.

Earlier attempts to deal with poverty

Monarchs before Elizabeth, including Henry VIII and Edward VI, passed laws that tried to deal with poverty, but the problem got worse.

- From 1495:
  - Beggars were punished in the **stocks** or sent back to their home towns.
- From 1531:
  - Beggars were publicly whipped.
  - Those caught a second time would have a hole burned in their ear.
  - A third offence would mean they were hanged.
- These laws remained in place for most of Elizabeth's reign.
- The 1576 'Act for setting the poor on work' placed the responsibility on local authorities.

Different authorities dealt with poverty in their own way.			
London	**York**	**Ipswich**	**Norwich**
• Bridewell Palace was used as a shelter for the homeless. • Bedlam hospital was built to house the mentally ill. • Other hospitals were opened for the sick and for orphans. • Conditions in all these institutions were poor and could not cope with the growing numbers coming to the city.	• In 1515, the city authority issued beggar licences, with a badge to identify holders. • From 1528, a Master Beggar was appointed to keep the others in order. • If beggars refused to work they were sent to the **House of Correction.**	• Introduced a licensing system for beggars from 1569. • Opened a hospital specifically to help the old and the sick. • A youth training scheme was introduced to help children learn a trade and escape poverty.	• After a survey showed that 80% of the population lived in poverty in 1570, the city authorities separated the poor into the 'idle poor' and the 'unfortunate poor'. • The 'idle poor' were given work such as knitting or sewing. The 'unfortunate poor' were given food and other forms of care. • Rich citizens were taxed to pay for the care of the vulnerable.

Government action: the Poor Law

In 1601, the first ever Poor Law was introduced. It stated that:

- The wealthy should be taxed to pay for the care of the sick and vulnerable.
- Fit and healthy paupers should be given work.
- Those who refused to work were still dealt with harshly: they could be whipped or placed in a House of Correction.

The poor were categorised into three groups:

The helpless poor (the sick and old): given food and accommodation.
The able-bodied poor (those considered fit): had to work in exchange for food.
The idle poor: punished and sent to a House of Correction.

How effective was the Poor Law?

Although the 1601 law did make a difference to some, it was not properly enforced in many areas. Begging seemed to decrease, but this may have been due to the threat of the House of Correction rather than the extra help available.

Some historians argue that the law was unsuccessful because it made each area responsible for its own paupers. Some were simply sent from one place to another without receiving any help.

SUMMARY

- Poverty was widespread in Elizabethan England for a variety of reasons, such as the closure of the monasteries, a larger population and changes in agriculture.

- Many wealthy Elizabethans felt duty-bound to help the poor and gave to charity. Almshouses were established in some areas.

- Paupers were generally seen as either deserving or undeserving.

- Paupers were usually dealt with harshly but some cities began to take a different, more practical approach.

- The 1601 Poor Law introduced a new approach nationally.

 APPLY

EXPLAIN

a Make a list of differences between the national approach to poverty before 1601 and the approaches taken in London, York, Ipswich and Norwich.

b **EXAM QUESTION** Explain what was important about how poverty was dealt with in cities like York, Ipswich and Norwich.

REVIEW

Look back at pages 28–30 to remind yourself about attitudes to the poor in Elizabethan times.

INTERPRETATION ANALYSIS

a Was the 1601 Poor Law a major change in Elizabethan attitudes to the poor? Make a list of arguments that say it was and arguments that say it wasn't.

b Read this interpretation about the Poor Law:

▼ **INTERPRETATION A** *Adapted from an article by the historian Marjorie K. McIntosh, published in the* Journal of Interdisciplinary History *in 2004:*

> The Elizabethan Poor Law extended throughout the country the best practices that had been developed over the last 20 years by pioneering towns. The law required that every parish should provide basic food, shelter, and clothing for the genuinely needy. However, the law was only applied to people who lived within the parish and exactly who would receive help and how it was to be given were left entirely up to parish officials. The Poor Laws also specified the forms of punishment for the idle or vagrant poor. When viewed in this light, England's so-called triumph in becoming the first European country to bring in poor relief in a nationwide policy looks rather less ambitious and certainly less noble.

- What view does the interpretation put forward about the 1601 Poor Law? Do you agree with the writer's argument?

c **EXAM QUESTION** How convincing is **Interpretation A** about the success of the 1601 Poor Law? Explain your answer using the interpretation and your contextual knowledge.

REVISION SKILLS

Highlight key points in the interpretation – use different colours for positive and negative – to help focus your analysis.

EXAMINER TIP

Remember to include specific details from the interpretation as well as your own knowledge.

CHAPTER 5

English sailors

Circumnavigation 1577–80

As well as a 'golden age', Elizabeth's reign has been called an 'age of discovery'. Although other countries, particularly Spain and Portugal, played a major role in exploring the world, it was England that led the way. Sailors like Sir Francis Drake, Sir Walter Raleigh and John Hawkins helped increase England's wealth and power with their voyages.

REVIEW

Hawkins's role in the age of discovery is covered on page 34.

Sir Francis Drake's circumnavigation

Between 1577 and 1580, Drake completed the first **circumnavigation** of the world in a single expedition.

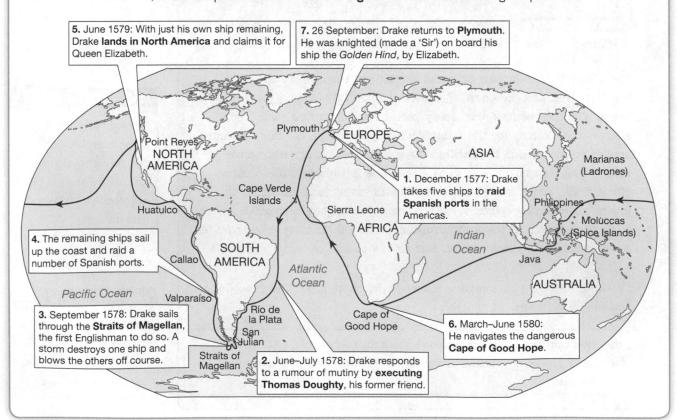

5. June 1579: With just his own ship remaining, Drake **lands in North America** and claims it for Queen Elizabeth.

7. 26 September: Drake returns to **Plymouth**. He was knighted (made a 'Sir') on board his ship the *Golden Hind*, by Elizabeth.

1. December 1577: Drake takes five ships to **raid Spanish ports** in the Americas.

4. The remaining ships sail up the coast and raid a number of Spanish ports.

3. September 1578: Drake sails through the **Straits of Magellan**, the first Englishman to do so. A storm destroys one ship and blows the others off course.

2. June–July 1578: Drake responds to a rumour of mutiny by **executing Thomas Doughty**, his former friend.

6. March–June 1580: He navigates the dangerous **Cape of Good Hope**.

Point Reyes
NORTH AMERICA
Huatulco
Callao
Valparaíso
Río de la Plata
San Julian
Straits of Magellan
SOUTH AMERICA
Cape Verde Islands
Plymouth
EUROPE
Sierra Leone
AFRICA
Cape of Good Hope
ASIA
Indian Ocean
Java
AUSTRALIA
Marianas (Ladrones)
Philippines
Moluccas (Spice Islands)
Pacific Ocean
Atlantic Ocean

Sir Walter Raleigh and the New World

- Sir Walter Raleigh was given royal permission to explore the Americas – the New World – in 1584.
- He would be allowed to **colonise** (take ownership of) any land that was not ruled by a Christian.
- In return, he had to give the queen one fifth of all the gold and silver he found there.
- He did not sail himself, but sent others to explore and establish colonies in the New World.
- A colony was established at Roanoke on the east coast of America but did not last. A second was created in 1587 and seemed like it was going to succeed. But when the colony's leader returned from a trip to England, he found all of the colonists gone and the word 'CROATOAN' (the name of a local tribe) carved into a tree!

Defences – better weapons such as cannons made it easier to explore hostile territory.

How was exploration possible?

Technology – better designed ships were much faster due to the triangular **lateen** sail.

Navigation – the **astrolabe** allowed sailors to judge their position, and more accurate compasses made navigation easier.

REVIEW

These developments also played a significant part in improvements to naval warfare – see page 52 for more on this.

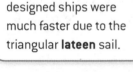 **APPLY**

EXPLAIN

a List three reasons why greater exploration was possible during Elizabeth's reign.

b How did improved navigation help voyages like Drake's?

WRITE AN ACCOUNT

a What did Drake achieve in 1577–80?

b Create a flow chart showing Drake's journey – use the map to help.

c **EXAM QUESTION** Write an account of Francis Drake's achievements during his circumnavigation.

EXAMINER TIP

For a 'write an account' question, you need to say why an event was important, not just tell the story.

The impact of voyages

Voyages by men like Drake, Raleigh and Hawkins brought England more wealth, power and territory.

John Hawkins and the slave trade

- John Hawkins was a respected sailor and courtier.
- He was responsible for building up the navy and commanding it against the Spanish Armada.
- In 1564, he kidnapped several hundred West Africans and sold them in South America. This was not the first example of the European slave trade, but it was the first time the whole process had been carried out by an Englishman.
- He was also a successful **privateer** and is thought to have brought tobacco to England.

A copy of John Hawkins' coat of arms

Wealth

Exploration allowed England to gain wealth in several ways:

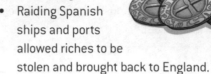

- Raiding Spanish ships and ports allowed riches to be stolen and brought back to England.
- Trading systems were established from which England's wealth grew over the following centuries and new products, like spices, silks and porcelain, were brought to England for the first time.
  - Trade with the East in spices and other goods grew as middlemen could now be cut out – English sailors could deal directly with merchants in Asia.
  - New companies were created to deal with trade in a particular area, for example, the Levant Company dealt exclusively with trade in Turkey and the Middle East.
  - The East India Company was established in 1600 to oversee trade in India and the Far East.
- The trade in African slaves brought significant wealth to individuals and to England as a whole. Other Englishmen saw how Hawkins had profited and so became involved in the slave trade over the following years. Slave labour enabled raw materials to be produced cheaply in the Americas.

REVIEW

To revise the events of the Armada, turn to pages 54–55.

Power

- Naval power had been growing under Elizabeth and was able to hold its own in any sea battle.
- Improved weapons and tactics, and the skilled command of men like Francis Drake, played a key role in this.
- The English victory over the Spanish Armada showed the dominant position that England held.

Territory

- England was not the first country to build colonies in newly discovered lands, and there were several failed attempts. But perseverance led to increasing numbers of colonies, particularly in North America, being established in the name of Queen Elizabeth and her successors.

SUMMARY

- The Elizabethan period was a time of great exploration.
- Sir Francis Drake, Sir Walter Raleigh and others discovered and explored new lands and brought wealth back to England.
- Trade was established in spices and other goods.
- The slave trade was established by John Hawkins and grew quickly during Elizabeth's reign.
- Exploration allowed England to gain in wealth, power and territory.

APPLY

INTERPRETATION ANALYSIS

a Make a list of reasons for exploration.

b Look at this interpretation about Elizabethan exploration:

▼ **INTERPRETATION A** *Adapted from a lecture given by Professor W.A. Neilson at Harvard University:*

> The peaceful development of England under the great Queen led to a need for wider markets, and besides the hope of plunder and the settlement of colonies, the Elizabethan merchant adventurers were seeking to build up a business overseas. Curiosity, patriotism, and trade were, then, the leading motives that led these daring 'sea dogs' on their perilous voyages to the ends of the earth.

- What does the interpretation suggest was the main purpose of exploration?

c
> **EXAM QUESTION** How convincing is **Interpretation A** about exploration in the Elizabethan period? Explain your answer using the interpretation and your contextual knowledge.

EXAMINER TIP

For this question, you need to consider how far the interpretation fits with your own knowledge of exploration. It might be useful to highlight or underline key elements of the text – you can do this in the exam too!

EXPLAIN

a Create a mind-map to show how voyages of exploration benefited England.

b
> **EXAM QUESTION** Explain what was important about the Elizabethan voyages of discovery.

EXAMINER TIP

For this question, you need to include all three of the different aspects in the boxes on these pages.

REVISION SKILLS

In the exam you will need to show knowledge of some key dates of the period. For this topic, it would useful to create an Exploration and Trade timeline, showing the key events that took place in the following years: 1564, 1580, 1587, 1600.

Religious matters

 **RECAP**

By 1558, England had undergone many years of dramatic religious change. The country had swung between Catholic and Protestant with each new monarch and Elizabeth wanted to bring calm and stability to the country.

CATHOLIC BELIEFS AND PRACTICES

- The **Pope** is the head of the Church.
- Bible and church services in Latin.
- Priests should not marry.
- Highly decorated churches.
- Bread and wine transform into body and blood of Jesus (transubstantiation).
- Priests are ordinary people's link with God.

PROTESTANT BELIEFS

- The monarch is the head of the Church.
- Bible and church services in English.
- Priests can marry.
- Plain churches.
- Bread and wine represent the body and blood.
- Ordinary people connect to God through prayer.

BOTH

- God created the world.
- Jesus was God's son.
- Those who challenge the true faith must be punished.

Elizabeth's religious settlement

Elizabeth was Protestant, but also practical — she knew that **compromise** would bring stability and peace.

Under Elizabeth:

- Priests were allowed to marry.
- Services were all in English and followed the Protestant **Book of Common Prayer**.
- She declared herself 'governor' rather than 'head' of the Church.
- Catholics could worship in their own way in private.
- A moderate Protestant, Matthew Parker, was appointed Archbishop of Canterbury.

Challenges to Elizabeth's religious settlement

1. The Northern Rebellion, 1569

Inspired by Elizabeth's refusal to allow the Duke of Norfolk to marry her Catholic cousin Mary, Queen of Scots, two northern nobles led a rebellion against Elizabeth. The Earl of Westmorland and the Earl of Northumberland took control of Durham Cathedral and held an illegal Catholic mass. They marched south with 4600 men but the rebels disbanded when the loyal Earl of Sussex raised an army against them. Northumberland was executed, Westmorland escaped to France and the Duke of Norfolk was imprisoned.

2. The papal bull, 1570

On 27 April 1570, Pope Pius V issued a special message (**papal bull**) in which he stated that Elizabeth was not the true queen and called on the people of England not to obey her laws. The bull also **excommunicated** her from the Church. The Pope's aim was to stir up rebellion by forcing English Catholics to choose between their queen or their religion.

3. The Ridolfi Plot, 1571

The plot was led by an Italian named Ridolfi, but also involved the Duke of Norfolk and a second northern rebellion. This time, the uprising would coincide with an invasion of foreign Catholics from the Netherlands and the murder of Queen Elizabeth. Her Catholic cousin, Mary, Queen of Scots, was to be placed on the throne and would marry the Duke of Norfolk. The plot was discovered before it could be carried out.

REVISION SKILLS

An important skill when revising is reducing lots of information into a clear, more concise form – this is sometimes known as 'chunking'. Go through the information on pages 36–37 and try to reduce it to no more than an A5 sheet.

APPLY

EXPLAIN

a Describe one similarity between Catholic and Protestant beliefs and practices.

b Describe three differences.

c **EXAM QUESTION** Explain what was important about Elizabeth's religious settlement.

EXAMINER TIP

For this question, you need to identify and explain why Elizabeth's religious settlement was a compromise.

WRITE AN ACCOUNT

a Create a storyboard that shows the three challenges Elizabeth faced as a result of her religious settlement.

b **EXAM QUESTION** Write an account of the early challenges to Elizabeth's religious settlement (1569–71).

EXAMINER TIP

Make sure you clearly show how the events you include in your answer were challenges to the religious settlement.

The 'Catholic threat'

Despite the failure of the Northern Rebellion and the Ridolfi Plot, Elizabeth continued to face challenges from some Catholics in England. Two further plots were uncovered in the 1580s:

The Throckmorton Plot, 1583

- Led by Sir Francis Throckmorton.

- The plan was to assassinate Elizabeth and replace her with Mary, Queen of Scots.

- There would then be an uprising of English Catholics and a French invasion. The Spanish ambassador was also involved.

- When the plot failed, Throckmorton was executed.

The Babington Plot, 1586

- Led by Anthony Babington.

- The plan was to murder Elizabeth and replace her with Mary, Queen of Scots.

- The plot's discovery led to the trial and execution of Mary.

REVIEW

The Babington Plot is covered in more detail on page 47.

The Counter-Reformation

The **Counter-Reformation** was the attempt by the Catholic Church to bring many Protestants back to the old faith. In 1568, William Allen established a **seminary** at Douai in the Netherlands to train Catholic priests. Allen aimed to send these priests to England as missionaries. He had the full backing of the Pope.

One key movement within the Counter-Reformation were the **Jesuits**.

Who were the Jesuits?

The Society of Jesus was created in 1540 and it began to send **missionaries** to England from 1580. Its purpose was to convert the Protestant population to Catholicism. Elizabeth saw the Jesuits as a threat.

Who were the key Jesuits in England?

Edmund Campion and Robert Parsons arrived in England on 24 June 1580 as missionaries. Campion travelled the country spreading his message, whereas Parsons kept a lower profile. Campion became a wanted man because the authorities were convinced he wanted to start a rebellion.

Were they really a threat?

Jesuits like Campion claimed not to want rebellion but just to spread their religious message. Elizabeth and many others, however, saw them as a genuine threat to the stability of England, even if they were not directly involved in any plots against her.

How serious was the Catholic threat to Elizabeth?

The **Pope** had made it very clear with his papal bull that he wanted Elizabeth's rule to end. He said it was the duty of Catholics to challenge her rule.

Jesuits and other missionaries were another serious threat as they could undermine the stability of her religious settlement.

European **Catholic rulers**, like Philip II of Spain, were encouraged by the Pope to challenge her authority.

English Catholics were encouraged by the papal bull to rebel.

⚙ APPLY

EXPLAIN

a   Create a list of the Catholic threats to Elizabeth after 1583.

b   What do you think was the greatest threat to Elizabeth's reign during this period?

INTERPRETATION ANALYSIS

a   Who were the Jesuits and what was their purpose?

b   Look at this interpretation about Robert Campion:

▼ **INTERPRETATION A** *Adapted from an article from Historyextra.com, first published 22 May 2015:*

'We travelled only for souls,' insisted Edmund Campion at his execution at Tyburn on 1 December 1581, 'we touched neither state nor policy.' These were indeed the instructions that this Jesuit and his accomplice, Robert Persons, had from Rome. But they were also armed with equipment to print books anonymously, they insisted that their followers did not attend Protestant services, and Campion challenged the state to a public debate.

Does the interpretation suggest that the Jesuits were a threat to Elizabeth?

c   **EXAM QUESTION** How convincing is **Interpretation A** about the Jesuits' aims in England? Explain your answer using the interpretation and your contextual knowledge.

EXAMINER TIP

For this question, make sure you include your wider knowledge of the Counter-Reformation and the Pope's response to Elizabeth's religious settlement.

Elizabeth's response to the 'Catholic threat' after 1580

 RECAP

A change in policy

In the 1580s, Elizabeth began to move away from the tolerance of Catholics that was part of her religious settlement. Instead she began to introduce increasingly anti-Catholic laws:

Date	Key points of law
1571	**Recusancy** fines for Catholics who did not take part in Protestant services. They could be fined or have property taken away. However, the rich could afford to pay and Elizabeth did not enforce the law too harshly; when Parliament tried to increase the fines, she resisted. It became illegal to own any Catholic items such as rosary beads.
1581	Recusancy fines were increased to £20 – more than most could afford; this law was strictly enforced. It became high treason to convert to Catholicism.
1585	Any Catholic priest who had been ordained (made a priest) after 1559 was considered a traitor and he, and anyone protecting him, faced death. It became legal to kill anyone who attempted to assassinate the queen.
1593	The 'statute of confinement' – Catholics could not travel more than five miles from home without permission from the authorities.

Dealing with the Jesuit threat

- **Campion:** By July 1580, Edmund Campion had spent a month travelling around England making speeches and encouraging people to convert to Catholicism. Elizabeth saw him as a threat to order and therefore to her. He was arrested and, despite maintaining that he had no plans to overthrow the queen, was brutally tortured and dragged through London before being hanged, drawn and quartered. It was clear that Elizabeth was not going to take any threat lightly.

 REVIEW

For a reminder about Campion and the Jesuits, look back at page 38.

- **Priests:** The 1585 Act Against Jesuits and Seminary priests called for them to be driven out of England. Many were executed.

The threat from abroad

Both Spain and France were powerful Catholic countries and invasion was a real concern for Elizabeth. The Spanish Armada of 1588 showed the fear was justified. The threat declined towards the end of her reign, following the Armada's defeat.

Powerful Catholics

Several powerful Catholic families lived in the north of England. They had mostly remained loyal, but there was growing concern that they might obey the Pope's command and rebel.

Why did Elizabeth's religious policy change?

Jesuit missionaries

The popularity of people like Campion undermined Elizabeth's authority. She could not allow them to spread their message.

The Ridolfi, Throckmorton and Babington Plots

Although these plots failed, they showed that Elizabeth had enemies who wanted to overthrow her and restore the Catholic Church.

 APPLY

EXPLAIN

a Summarise Edmund Campion's life and death in no more than 30 words.

b **EXAM QUESTION** Explain what was important about Catholic missionaries to England after 1574.

EXAMINER TIP

In your answer, you need to explain the background and purpose of Campion's mission and the reason for his arrest and execution. You should then explain what this tells you about religion in Elizabethan England.

WRITE AN ACCOUNT

a Create a set of flashcards about the new laws that Elizabeth passed between 1571 and 1593.

b Why were these laws passed? Use your contextual knowledge to help answer this question.

c **EXAM QUESTION** Write an account of how Elizabeth's policy towards Catholicism changed in the 1580s.

EXAMINER TIP

For this question, make sure you write about more than one change in Elizabeth's policy.

Puritans and their beliefs

Who were the Puritans?

- Strict Protestants who were influenced by extreme Protestants in Europe, like John Calvin.

- In some cases, they lived in **exile** in Europe during the reign of Elizabeth's Catholic sister, Mary.

- They were keen to remove all Catholic elements from the English Church.

- They studied the Bible, wanted plain clothing and simple services.

- Some Puritans were appointed as bishops by Elizabeth, though some argued over their robes. By 1568, most of them had agreed to wear the white gown or **surplice** required by the Church of England during services.

Hard-line Puritans

Known as **Presbyterians**, they questioned Elizabeth's religious settlement and the need for bishops.

→

In the 1570s, they held popular meetings, called **prophesyings**, to discuss the Bible. There was often criticism of the queen and her religious policies at these meetings, too.

Elizabeth suspended Grindal as Archbishop.

←

Edmund Grindal, the Archbishop of Canterbury, encouraged prophesyings, despite these criticisms.

In 1580, John Field, a prominent and very strict Puritan, was banned from preaching.

→

The leaders of a new **separatist** church founded in London in 1593, Henry Barrow and John Greenwood, were hanged.

Powerful Puritans

A number of Puritans with less strict views were able rise to powerful positions:

- **Sir Francis Walsingham** — the queen's senior minister and spymaster. He largely kept his religious views to himself, aware they might make him unpopular.

- **Robert Dudley, Earl of Leicester** — a privy councillor and seen as a potential husband for Elizabeth. He was unwilling to put his position at risk by openly challenging the Church.

- **Peter Wentworth and Anthony Cope** — Presbyterian MPs who tried to bring change to the Church by introducing bills to Parliament, however, they did not gain much support from other MPs.

Elizabeth's response to Puritanism

When Grindal died in 1583, Elizabeth replaced him as Archbishop with John Whitgift, who took a tough stance against Puritans. With this key appointment, and the deaths of Dudley in 1588 and Walsingham in 1590, Elizabeth began to crack down on Puritanism.

Measures against Puritans included:

- New rules introduced by Whitgift banning unlicensed preaching and forcing church attendance with recusancy fines.

- A new High Commission with the power to fine and imprison Puritans who refused to follow the rules.

- The dismissal or imprisonment of hundreds of clergymen.

- The punishment of printers for spreading the Puritan message.

- A crackdown on high profile Puritans, like Anthony Cope, who was imprisoned in the Tower of London.

> The Church of England had brought stability to religion and people were unwilling to risk losing it.

> The death of powerful Puritans removed its influence in the royal court.

> **Why did the influence of Puritanism decline after 1590?**

> Whitgift's crackdown broke the organisation of Puritanism.

> The death of John Field in 1588 – this important leader had inspired many and been highly critical of the Church of England.

 **APPLY**

WRITE AN ACCOUNT

a Create a spider diagram of the main beliefs and practices of Puritanism.

b Write definitions for the following terms:

- Presbyterian
- prophesying
- separatist.

c **EXAM QUESTION** Write an account of the ways in which Puritans challenged the Elizabethan Church.

EXAMINER TIP

Make sure you include the fact that a significant number of Puritans did accept the religious changes – they did not all become hard-liners.

EXPLAIN

a What was Archbishop Grindal's approach to Puritanism?

b How did this change under Archbishop Whitgift?

c **EXAM QUESTION** Explain the importance of Archbishop John Whitgift in the decline of Puritanism in Elizabethan England.

EXAMINER TIP

To show how important Whitgift was, you need to explain the situation before and after his appointment.

The failure of rebellions against Elizabeth

There were several plots and rebellions against Elizabeth's rule. The reasons behind these can be split into two categories:

Religion (the most common cause): for example, the Northern Rebellion and the Babington Plot. These were usually based on the belief that Elizabeth had no right to be queen, and had the aim of replacing her with Mary, Queen of Scots.

Power and influence: for example, the Essex Rebellion. This was the result of rivalries within the Privy Council and the battle for influence over the queen.

REVIEW

For a reminder of Essex's rebellion go to page 20, and for more on the Catholic plots and rebellions look back at pages 35–38.

Regardless of what was behind the plots and rebellions, all of them had one thing in common: they failed! The Ridolfi, Throckmorton and Babington Plots were discovered before they were put into action, while the Northern Rebellion in 1569 and Essex's rebellion in 1601 were quickly defeated.

Spies

- Elizabeth's huge network of spies was able to quickly identify threats and deal with troublemakers.
- Sir Francis Walsingham, one of the queen's most trusted advisors, was also her spymaster.

A skilled politician

- Elizabeth was good at getting her own way.
- She dealt with Parliament with great skill, allowing MPs and lords to feel that they had influence while still showing who had the final say.

Why did plots against Elizabeth fail?

Unconvincing alternatives

- Most people, even Catholics, preferred the idea of an English queen to a foreign ruler like Mary, Queen of Scots, or Philip II of Spain.
- Mary was not generally trusted, having been widely blamed for her husband's death, and Philip, who had been crowned King of England after marrying Elizabeth's sister, Mary, had shown little interest in the country. His wife had sent hundreds of Protestants to be burnt at the stake.
- The lack of a popular alternative monarch meant that most rebellions could not gain wide support.

Punishment

- Elizabeth rarely showed mercy to those who betrayed her.
- Rebels were tortured and brutally executed.
- Elizabeth even executed her own cousin, Mary, Queen of Scots, and her former favourite, the Earl of Essex.
- For potential rebels, the consequences were clear to see.

Religious settlement

- Elizabeth's religious policy kept the majority happy.
- Although there were crackdowns on Catholics and Puritans later in her reign, religious differences were mostly tolerated.

SUMMARY

- Elizabeth brought stability to England through her religious settlement – a Protestant Church but with some compromises. Catholics were largely allowed to practise their religion in private.

- The Pope excommunicated Elizabeth in 1570 and called on Catholics to challenge her role. This led to several plots and rebellions and an increased threat from Catholic powers like Spain and France. Jesuit missionaries tried to convert the English.

- In response, Elizabeth treated Catholics more harshly.

- Puritanism became increasingly popular in England and was allowed, or even encouraged, by powerful men at court and in the Church.

- After 1590, there was a crackdown on Puritans.

- Elizabeth was able to maintain her power by dealing effectively with those who challenged her. Plots were either discovered early or quickly defeated.

REVISION SKILLS

It is vital that you have a good understanding of the chronology of the religious changes and challenges of Elizabeth's reign. Go back through this chapter and record key dates on a set of cards. Record the events and developments on another set and then test yourself by matching them up.

APPLY

WRITE AN ACCOUNT

a   What were the two main causes of plots and rebellions against Elizabeth's rule?

b   Copy and complete this table. Use Chapter 2 and the first section of this chapter to help you.

Plot or rebellion?	What happened?	Why did it fail?

c   **EXAM QUESTION** Write an account of how Elizabeth dealt with plots and rebellions against her rule.

EXPLAIN

a   Make a set of flashcards – one for each of the reasons why plots and rebellions against Elizabeth failed.

b   Rearrange the cards in order of importance – which was the most important reason for the failure of rebellions? Which was the least important?

c   **EXAM QUESTION** Explain what was important about the advantages Queen Elizabeth had over those plotting against her.

EXAMINER TIP

You need to explain why Elizabeth had advantages that would make it difficult for plotters to gain wider support.

CHAPTER 7

Mary, Queen of Scots

Who was Mary, Queen of Scots?

Mary, Queen of Scots, was a major figure in Elizabeth's reign for several reasons:

- Elizabeth's cousin. Her grandmother was Henry VIII's sister.

- A Catholic.

- Became Queen of Scotland in 1542, at only eight-days-old.

- Married the heir to the French throne in 1558 and was briefly queen of two countries.

- As Elizabeth had no children, Mary was also heir to the throne of England, some believed she was in fact the rightful queen.

- After her husband's death, she returned to Scotland but became increasingly unpopular. Scotland had become increasingly Protestant in her absence.

- In 1567, having been accused of the murder of her second husband, Lord Darnley, Mary fled to England. Her young son, James, was crowned King of Scotland in her place.

The 'threat'

Mary's arrival in England concerned many Protestants. They were worried that she might directly lead, or simply inspire, a rebellion against Elizabeth. The idea that she could ever become queen reminded them of the horrors of Mary I's reign. Parliament and a number of privy councillors called for Mary's execution, but Elizabeth was hesitant. She did not want to kill a fellow queen. Mary was kept under close guard and moved around England for the next 19 years. Although she was not directly involved in plots against Elizabeth, she was certainly an inspiration for several. One final plot in 1586 did seem to involve Mary directly.

REVIEW

Look back at pages 36–38 to remind yourself about some of the plots against Elizabeth. In particular, focus on the Northern Rebellion and the Ridolfi Plot.

The Babington Plot

The plotter

In 1586, a rich young Catholic named Anthony Babington planned to kill Elizabeth, rescue Mary and place her on the throne.

The plot

Babington needed to know if Mary supported his plan. He managed to get Mary's servants to hide coded messages within beer barrels that were sent to her room. The messages reached Mary and she replied, giving her backing to the plot.

The plot uncovered

Unfortunately for Mary, the servants were spies for Sir Francis Walsingham, Elizabeth's spymaster. The original message and Mary's reply were decoded and taken straight to Elizabeth. It was clear that Mary was plotting to kill the queen.

The aftermath

With such clear evidence, Elizabeth had little choice but to act. Although still hesitant, she ordered that Mary should go on trial for treason.

 APPLY

EXPLAIN

a   Create a flow chart to show how Mary came to be in England in 1568.

b   Why did her arrival concern many Protestants?

REVISION SKILLS

Remember that the exam rewards you for accurate spelling, punctuation and grammar (SPaG) — make sure you get into good habits as you revise!

WRITE AN ACCOUNT

a   Describe the events of the Babington Plot in 50 words. Now try to describe it in 20 words.

b   **EXAM QUESTION** Write an account of the ways in which the Babington Plot affected Elizabeth's policy towards Mary, Queen of Scots.

EXAMINER TIP

For this question, don't just describe the Babington Plot; you need to say why it was significant in the story of Mary, Queen of Scots.

 **RECAP**

Elizabeth's treatment of Mary, Queen of Scots

The trial

- In October 1586, Mary was put on trial before a court of 36 noblemen including Sir Francis Walsingham and Sir William Cecil, two of Elizabeth's closest advisors.
- Mary defended herself strongly. She criticised the fact that she had not been allowed to see evidence against her and claimed that as she was not English, she could not be guilty of treason. She refused to accept that the court had any right to pass sentence on her.
- She was found guilty and sentenced to death on 25 October.

The execution

- Elizabeth was reluctant to sign Mary's death warrant. She feared that executing a fellow monarch might inspire her enemies, or that Mary's son James might want revenge.
- She was also concerned about the reaction of the Catholic powers: France and Spain.
- Despite this, she signed the death warrant on 1 February 1587.
- Mary was executed, in private, seven days later at Fotheringhay Castle. The Earls of Shrewsbury and Kent were the official witnesses.

The impact

- Without Mary, Catholics had no clear alternative monarch. The new heir to the English throne was Mary's son James – a Protestant.
- Even in death, Mary remained an important figure. Many saw her as a **martyr** to her faith and her execution as proof that Elizabeth was a wicked heretic.
- Elizabeth's concern about the reaction abroad was unwarranted – there was outrage but no action from France or Spain. King James of Scotland accepted Elizabeth's apology for the death of his mother.

Timeline

▼ 1542
- Born and became Queen of Scotland

▼ 1558
- Married heir to the French throne

▼ 1561
- Returned to Scotland, following the King of France's death

▼ 1565
- Married Lord Darnley

▼ 1566
- Birth of her son, James (later King James VI of Scotland and James I of England)

▼ 1567
- Forced to abdicate following the murder of Lord Darnley

1568
- Escaped to England

▼ 1586
- Went on trial for treason

▼ 1587
- Executed

SUMMARY

- Mary, Queen of Scots, arrived in England in 1567 and was immediately seen as a threat to Elizabeth's throne and the religious settlement.
- She was not directly involved in plots but was a clear inspiration for the Northern Rebellion, the Ridolfi Plot and others.
- After agreeing to take part in the Babington Plot she was put on trial, and executed in 1587.
- Her death removed the direct threat to Elizabeth, but she remained a symbol to Catholics as a martyr to their faith.

APPLY

INTERPRETATION ANALYSIS

a Look at this interpretation about Mary, Queen of Scots:

▼ **INTERPRETATION A** *Adapted from* Elizabeth in Danger *by S. M. Harrison, 1984:*

> Mary's presence in England created grave problems, and Elizabeth's worst fears about Mary soon proved to be real. Francis Walsingham wanted to end the danger posed by Mary once and for all. However, he realised that Elizabeth would not consent to execution until she was convinced by positive proof that Mary was actually involved in a plot against her life. To this day historians argue about Mary's guilt or innocence.
>
> In London the news of Mary's death was greeted with joy. Elizabeth, however, seemed furious. She said the execution was a mistake. Possibly this was true, but with Mary, Queen of Scots was dead, the Catholic threat was now even greater. Philip of Spain had never been enthusiastic about invading England on Mary's behalf but in her will, Mary gave Philip her title to the English throne.

- Why did Mary's arrival pose problems for Queen Elizabeth?

  _____
  _____
  _____

- What positive proof did Walsingham supply?

  _____
  _____

- Why might Elizabeth have seen the execution as a mistake?

  _____
  _____
  _____
  _____
  _____

b **EXAM QUESTION** How convincing is **Interpretation A** about Mary, Queen of Scots? Explain your answer using the interpretation and your contextual knowledge.

EXPLAIN

a Create a storyboard showing the key events of Mary's life between her arrival in England and her death.

b **EXAM QUESTION** Explain the importance of the execution of Mary, Queen of Scots.

CHAPTER 8

Conflict with Spain

Reasons and events

At this time, Catholic Spain was one of the richest and most powerful countries in the world. However, during Elizabeth's reign, growing tension between England and Spain would eventually lead to war.

The issue of marriage

- King Philip II of Spain had been married to Elizabeth's sister, Mary I. During this time, he had been joint monarch of England. The plan was that their child would unite England and Spain under one Catholic king or queen. When Mary died childless in November 1558, so did the plan.
- Philip proposed to Elizabeth in 1559, but, as with many other suitors, she kept him waiting for an answer. As it became clear that the marriage would not take place, tensions between the countries grew.

The papal bull

- In 1570, the Pope excommunicated Elizabeth and called for all Catholics to challenge her rule. As a Catholic, Philip was keen to follow the Pope's instructions.

Why was there conflict between Spain and England?

Religious difference

- Elizabeth had returned England to the Protestant faith after the Catholic years of Mary I (1553–58). Spain had remained Catholic throughout all the religious changes of the Reformation. Such opposing religious ideas led to conflict.

The actions of sailors

- Sir Francis Drake and other English sailors had spent years raiding Spanish ports and ships, and stealing treasures from Spanish colonies in South America and closer to home. The most notable example was in 1587 when Drake led a raid on the port of Cadiz. He destroyed dozens of Spanish ships in what became known as 'singeing the King of Spain's beard'.
- Elizabeth encouraged these acts by granting licences in exchange for sharing the treasures with the country.

REVISION SKILLS

Break down the information for the topic you are revising in different ways. You can create a brief fact file containing two or three important points about key people or events.

REVIEW

Look back at pages 33–35 for more information about English sailors such as Sir Francis Drake, Sir Walter Raleigh and John Hawkins.

The Netherlands

- As well as Spain, Philip also ruled the Netherlands. In 1566, there was a Protestant uprising in the country. Philip sent troops to restore order but this led to even greater resistance from the rebels.
- Although she wanted to avoid war with Spain, Elizabeth agreed to send money to support the Protestants and allowed English volunteers to go and help in the fight. She also let rebel ships use English ports. All of this angered Philip greatly.
- William of Orange, the Dutch rebel leader, was assassinated in 1584. In December 1585, Elizabeth finally agreed to send English troops to support her fellow Protestants. She sent her trusted friend Robert Dudley with 7000 soldiers. Dudley and his men had very little impact but it was a clear act of war against Spain.

 APPLY

EXPLAIN

a Make a set of revision cards to help you learn the reasons for conflict between England and Spain. You could use colour to categorise them using the following headings.

- Royal marriage
- The Pope
- Religious difference
- Sailors
- The Netherlands

b Using your cards, place the reasons for conflict in order of importance.

c Explain what was important about events in the Netherlands for relations between England and Spain.

EXAMINER TIP

For this question, make sure you refer to the ways in which Elizabeth's actions in the Netherlands would have worsened relations between England and Spain.

WRITE AN ACCOUNT

a Can you identify any turning points in relations between England and Spain? When did the relationship begin to deteriorate?

b Write an account of the growing conflict between England and Spain from 1568 to 1587.

EXAMINER TIP

Always be clear on what to include when there are dates within a question – the Spanish Armada falls outside of these dates and so you should not include it in your answer.

Naval warfare

During Elizabeth's reign, the seas were dominated by three powerful countries: England, Spain and France. Their superiority relied on three things: the size of their fleet, tactics and technology.

The size of the fleet

Henry VIII had spent a fortune building a huge navy to protect his island nation. Before 1500, ships had simply been a way to get to battle, but Tudor ships were designed to fight. During Elizabeth's reign, under the command of John Hawkins, England's navy continued to grow. At the same time, Philip of Spain spared no expense in trying to make his navy the largest and most powerful in the world.

Tactics

- When full scale battles were fought, a tactic called the **line of battle** was sometimes used. Ships formed into a single line and fired together on the enemy. The aim was to sink as many as possible.
- **Raids** were a common form of attack. They took enemy ports by surprise and destroyed as many ships as possible before the enemy had the chance to fight back. This kind of attack also allowed for treasure to be stolen.
- **Fireships** were an effective tactic used in the sixteenth century. An old ship would be set alight and sent into the middle of the enemy fleet. This would send panic across the wooden ships and cause great damage at little risk to the attacker.

REVIEW

You might want to look back at pages 34–35 or forward to pages 54–55 to help you understand how these tactics worked in practice.

Technology

- A new type of triangular sail, known as a lateen, allowed for much faster travel and new ships allowed for greater speed and manoeuvrability. Ships could therefore travel greater distances and perform better in raids and battles.
- New, more powerful, **cannons** meant it was now possible to fire at enemy ships from a distance. Previously, sailors would try to board enemy ships. Ships were built specifically for battle and for use in the line of battle tactic.
- New inventions like the astrolabe allowed for greater accuracy when planning voyages and working out locations. This helped sailors prepare much better for long voyages, particularly if they had to pass through hostile waters.

 **APPLY**

EXPLAIN

a Create a mind-map of the key features of naval warfare in the sixteenth century.

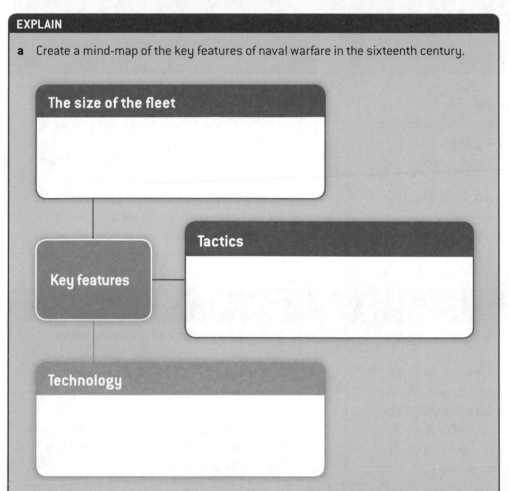

The size of the fleet

Tactics

Key features

Technology

b Which do you think was the most important development and why?

c **EXAM QUESTION** Explain what was important about new technology in the development of naval warfare in sixteenth-century England.

EXAMINER TIP

Remember to describe the developments with specific detail as well as explaining their importance.

WRITE AN ACCOUNT

a Who was responsible for the growth of the navy under Elizabeth's reign?

b Make a list of the ways in which naval warfare developed under Elizabeth.

REVISION SKILLS

Remember each type of exam question asks you to do something different with your knowledge. You may be asked to explain *why* countries saw naval strength as important. Make sure you are able to answer.

The Spanish Armada

1: The plan

- In 1588, Philip II of Spain launched his great Armada: 151 ships, 7000 sailors and 34,000 soldiers would sail to the Netherlands and collect more men before invading England.
- They would sail in an unbreakable crescent formation.
- Philip was so confident that he would defeat the English navy that he filled the ships with weapons for land battles that would follow once the fleet arrived in England.

2: The English strike first

- By 6 August the Armada was anchored off the Dutch coast.
- They were delayed for several days waiting for additional soldiers to arrive.
- At this moment the English, commanded by Sir Francis Drake, chose to strike. Early on 7 August, eight fireships were sent into the Spanish fleet. There was mass panic and the well-organised Armada was plunged into chaos.

4: The storm

- A great storm blew the retreating Armada way off course.
- Their food rotten, their water polluted and with no maps for the waters around northern Britain, many ships were wrecked. Survivors who made it to shore were slaughtered by the Scots or the Irish.
- Of 151 ships, only 65 returned to Spain.

3: The battle

- On 8 August the Battle of Gravelines began.
- The English fired constantly from a distance of 100 metres. The Spanish ships were badly damaged but none were sunk.
- Recognising how bad the situation was, the Spanish commander, the Duke of Medina-Sidonia, tried to lead his battered ships home. The English gave chase.

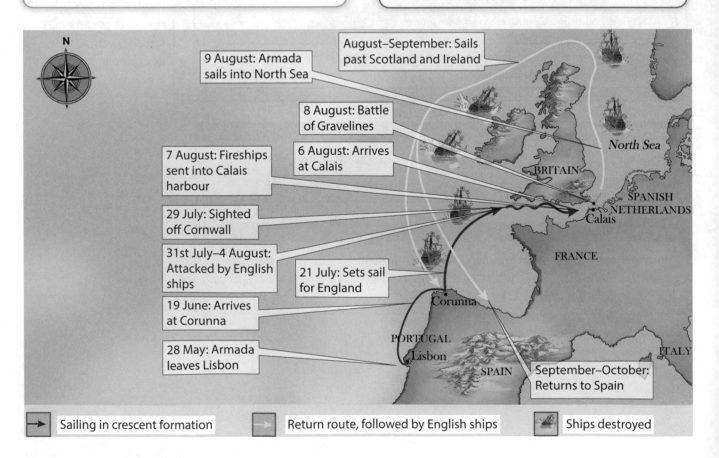

August–September: Sails past Scotland and Ireland

9 August: Armada sails into North Sea

8 August: Battle of Gravelines

7 August: Fireships sent into Calais harbour

6 August: Arrives at Calais

29 July: Sighted off Cornwall

31st July–4 August: Attacked by English ships

21 July: Sets sail for England

19 June: Arrives at Corunna

28 May: Armada leaves Lisbon

September–October: Returns to Spain

North Sea
BRITAIN
SPANISH NETHERLANDS
Calais
FRANCE
Corunna
PORTUGAL
Lisbon
SPAIN
ITALY

→ Sailing in crescent formation
→ Return route, followed by English ships
Ships destroyed

English tactics

- The fireships broke the formation of the fleet and made individual ships vulnerable to attack.
- The bombardment by the English cannons made regrouping impossible.
- The English had faster ships and more experienced and skilled commanders.

How was the Armada defeated?

Spanish mistakes

- Spanish ships were designed for the Mediterranean and could not cope with the harsh conditions of the English Channel and the North Sea.
- They were delayed in the Netherlands because the soldiers were not ready to board.
- Their weapons were mostly for land use, leaving them almost defenceless at sea. They had also brought many of the wrong cannonballs.
- The commander of the fleet was inexperienced.

The weather

- Storms caused great destruction to the Spanish fleet.
- The storms delayed their return to Spain, meaning that their food and water went off or ran out. Many sailors became too sick to sail.

The consequences of the defeat of the Armada

The Armada's defeat was a great victory for Elizabeth. It proved that England was a major naval power. The country could not rest, however. Invasion remained a concern and Philip quickly began planning a second attempt, but he never actually tried again. Elizabeth continued to strengthen her navy.
The Armada had brought England together. Under threat of foreign invasion, most Catholics had declared their total loyalty to Elizabeth. It made Elizabeth even more popular and respected as a leader, and helped boost the idea of the 'Golden Age'.

SUMMARY

- England and Spain were both significant naval powers and bitter rivals.
- There were several reasons for their conflict, mostly based around religious difference – England was Protestant and Spain was Catholic. Conflict in the Netherlands increased tension between the countries.
- Naval warfare developed greatly during Elizabeth's reign due to growing fleets and improved tactics and technology.
- The Spanish Armada, launched against England in 1588, failed for several reasons.
- Its failure established England as a major naval power.

 APPLY

WRITE AN ACCOUNT

a Make a timeline of the key events of the Spanish Armada. Use the map to help you.

b **EXAM QUESTION** Write an account of the failure of the Spanish attempt to invade England in 1588.

 EXAMINER TIP
Select a couple of turning points in the story of the Armada that will help account for the failure mentioned in the question.

HISTORIC ENVIRONMENT

a Explain the reasons for the Armada's defeat in your own words.

b Which was the most important reason? Explain your answer.

c **EXAM QUESTION** 'Superior tactics were the most important factor in the outcome of battles at sea during Elizabeth's reign.' How far does a study of the Spanish Armada support this statement? Explain your answer. You should refer to both the Spanish Armada and your contextual knowledge.

 EXAMINER TIP
Don't just write down everything you know about the Armada. You need to focus on why the Spanish were defeated.

Exam practice

GCSE sample answers

On these exam practice pages, you will find a sample student answers for each of the question types in the Elizabethan England section of your Paper 2 exam. What are the strengths and weaknesses of the answers? Read the following pages and think carefully about what the student has written, what the examiner has said about each answer, and how you might improve your own answers.

The 'interpretation' question

▼ **INTERPRETATION C** *Adapted from* Elizabeth I and the Puritans *by William Haller, published in 1972:*

> Those Puritans led and organised by Cartwright and Field posed a formidable challenge not only to the authority of the bishops but to the queen herself. The Puritans also had many supporters, not only in Parliament but among the queen's own advisors and courtiers. Lord Burghley, her wisest and most trusted councillor, the Earl of Leicester, her favourite, Sir Francis Walsingham, her principal secretary, all inclined to some degree to the Puritan side.

 EXAM QUESTION How convincing is **Interpretation C** about the threat posed by the Puritans during the reign of Elizabeth I? Explain your answer using **Interpretation C** and your contextual knowledge.

8 marks

Sample student answer

Interpretation C describes the challenge that Puritanism was to Elizabeth. It is convincing because it states that some Puritans led by Thomas Cartwright and John Field posed a clear threat to her authority. In the 1570s, Field emerged as a leading preacher in London. He called for a complete overhaul of the Church of England in his book 'A View of the Popish Abuses Yet Remaining in the English Church', which called into question the whole of Elizabeth's religious settlement. Field was arrested and imprisoned for a year and, following his release, was banned from preaching. His escape from more severe punishment was probably due to the influence of powerful Puritans in the queen's inner circle.

The fact that the interpretation names a number of key figures in Elizabeth's court, including Sir Francis Walsingham and Robert Dudley, also makes it convincing.

The presence of so many key privy councillors with Puritan sympathies meant that Puritan ideas might influence the queen and her policies more than other Protestant ideas. As some Puritans were extreme, like Field, and attacked the bishops who were appointed by the queen, this was a threat to her authority, because Elizabeth was in charge of the Church, and criticism of

 EXAMINER TIP

This first paragraph contains detailed contextual knowledge that shows a wider understanding of the period.

 EXAMINER TIP

Providing some detail on Thomas Cartwright (who is specifically mentioned in the interpretation) would improve this answer.

 EXAMINER TIP

The answer relates to the question by using the word 'convincing', and uses historical knowledge to back up the idea that it is convincing.

 EXAMINER TIP

This part of the answer shows a relevance to the idea of 'threat' in the question.

the Church was criticism of her. Fortunately, the Puritans close to the queen were moderate and, as the interpretation says, were only 'inclined to some degree'.

EXAMINER TIP

This answer could be developed by suggesting what effects Puritan influence at court and in the Privy Council might have had.

OVERALL COMMENT

This answer is largely a Level 3 response, but shows some elements of Level 4. It offers a developed evaluation of the interpretation and includes a good level of contextual knowledge. It shows an understanding of more than one aspect of the interpretation.

OVER TO YOU

1   A big part of successfully answering an 'interpretation' question is showing a good level of knowledge. The key skill is knowing which bits of knowledge are relevant.

   a   Use pages 42–43 of this revision guide to create a mind-map on the Puritans.

   b   Now highlight the contextual knowledge that would be useful in answering this question.

2   Reread the first paragraph of the answer.

   a   Write down two positive features and one area for improvement for this section.

   b   Rewrite the paragraph incorporating your improvements.

3   Have a go at writing your own answer to the question (allow yourself a maximum of 10 minutes). When you have answered a question like this, ask yourself the following:

   a   Have you shown that you understand the interpretation?

   b   Have you said whether the interpretation fits with your knowledge of the period?

   c   Have you made a judgement about whether it is 'convincing'?

The 'explain' question

EXAM QUESTION Explain what was important about voyages abroad in the reign of Elizabeth I.

8 marks

Sample student answer

The Elizabethan era saw voyages and exploration around the globe. The voyages were important for several reasons. The primary aim for many of the voyages was increased wealth. Sailors like Sir Francis Drake brought riches back to England by raiding Spanish ships and ports. These raids could also be used to embarrass enemies, as was the case with Drake's raid on the Spanish port of Cadiz in 1587 – 'singeing the King of Spain's beard'.

   In addition to raids, money could also be made through trade. Voyages abroad allowed new trade routes to be established to the Far East. This brought

EXAMINER TIP

Specific detail about the raid on Cadiz shows good knowledge of the period.

spices and other exotic goods to England. John Hawkins established the first trade in African slaves, a trade that not only provided great wealth for him personally but also for England. New technology, such as the astrolabe, allowed for more accurate navigation, and the development of the lateen sail and improved ship design allowed for greater speed and manoeuvrability.

A second reason why voyages abroad were so important in Elizabethan England was that they increased the country's territory. The first attempt to establish a colony in North America was unsuccessful and Spain and Portugal had beaten England in the race to colonise South America.

Voyages abroad were important because of the wealth they brought back to England and the power that they projected to rival nations. They were also important because they laid the foundations for the dominance of the sea, trade and colonies that would grow after the end of Elizabeth's reign. Voyages abroad also helped to establish the idea of 'Gloriana' and the Elizabethan Golden Age.

EXAMINER TIP

More specific detailed knowledge to support the analysis that voyages increased the country's territory would have been better here.

EXAMINER TIP

Reference to Gloriana and the 'Golden Age' places voyages abroad into the wider historical context.

OVERALL COMMENT

This answer would achieve Level 3. It shows a good level of contextual knowledge. It explains some of the consequences of the voyages for England but would gain further merit if it were to explain the broader consequences, and with more precise knowledge to support it.

OVER TO YOU

1 How would you improve the sample answer?

 a Highlight in one colour the key points at which the question is answered.

 b Highlight in another colour anything that you think is not directly relevant to the question.

 c Imagine you are the examiner: write down two strengths of this answer and two areas for improvement.

2 Now have a go at writing your own answer to the question using the sentence starters below. Allow yourself a maximum of 10 minutes to complete this task.

 In the Elizabethan era voyages abroad were …

 One reason for their importance was …

 A second reason was …

 Overall, they were important because …

3 Now check your answer:

 a Have you explained what made the event important?

 b Have you included a range of detailed knowledge?

REVIEW

Before you tackle the question, take time to refresh your knowledge about voyages during Elizabeth's reign by rereading pages 32–35.

The 'write an account' question

 EXAM QUESTION Write an account of how the Earl of Essex lost Queen Elizabeth's favour.

8 marks

Sample student answer

In 1601, the Earl of Essex, one of the queen's former favourites, started a rebellion against her. For the majority of Elizabeth's reign, Essex was one of her most trusted advisors. Some saw him as a potential husband and Elizabeth certainly took an interest in him when he arrived at court in 1587. He became a privy councillor in 1595 and grew even more powerful when he was given the monopoly of sweet wine in England. His military successes against the Spanish improved his standing even further. He developed a rivalry with Robert Cecil, although Essex remained more popular with the queen. Just a few years after he reached the height of his success, however, Essex fell dramatically from favour.

In 1598, Essex became involved in an argument with the queen at a Privy Council meeting. In temper, he turned his back on her and she responded by hitting him on the head. Essex almost drew his sword but was stopped by others. He was sent to Ireland where he was given the task of crushing the rebellion. Essex not only failed to defeat the rebels but made a peace treaty with their leader – directly going against the queen's orders. He also disobeyed the queen by knighting many of his close friends. To make matters worse, when he returned to England he rushed straight in to see Elizabeth and caught her without her wig. This not only cost Essex his influence in court but also his money, as Elizabeth refused to renew his sweet wine monopoly. In this way, the Earl of Essex lost the queen's favour.

Financially ruined, Essex completed his fall from favour by rebelling against the queen. These actions could not go unpunished, and Essex was executed.

 EXAMINER TIP

The opening sentences show a clear understanding of the question by establishing why Essex had the queen's favour.

 EXAMINER TIP

It would have been good to go into more detail about the Privy Council and the system of monopolies, to show an understanding of the key features of the period.

 EXAMINER TIP

The answer includes dates to show specific knowledge of the period.

OVERALL COMMENT

This would be a Level 3 answer. It shows a good understanding of the sequence of events of Essex's rebellion and therefore demonstrates a good knowledge of the key features and characteristics of the period. There is some analysis and explanation. To achieve Level 4, the answer should show some knowledge of the importance of the royal court, patronage and loyalty, as this would put Essex's disgrace into a broader context.

OVER TO YOU

1   For this question, you need to show good knowledge of why what Essex did would cause the queen to look unfavourably on him. How well do you think the answer does this? Can you identify the reasons given? Has anything been missed out?

2   Using the advice given here and your own feedback on the answer, rewrite the answer to improve it. Spend no more than 10 minutes on this.

3   Now check your answer:

    a   Have you shown how one event led to another?

    b   Have you included plenty of historical detail?

    c   Have you shown a wider knowledge of the period?

The 'historic environment' question

EXAM QUESTION 'One of the main reasons for building stately homes in Elizabethan times was to show the wealth and status of the owner.' How far does a study of Hardwick Hall support this statement? Explain your answer. You should refer to Hardwick Hall and your contextual knowledge.

16 marks

Sample student answer

For rich Elizabethans, the building of grand country houses offered the opportunity to show off their wealth and demonstrate the position that they held in society. Hardwick Hall in Derbyshire, built by Bess of Hardwick, is a clear example of this.

Although born into the gentry, Bess of Hardwick rose through Elizabethan society due to her marriages to important and powerful figures in the Tudor court, finally marrying the Earl of Shrewsbury in 1567 and becoming a member of the nobility. A house was needed that reflected her social position and Hardwick Hall was built. Each part of the building was specifically designed to show her status, wealth and cultured tastes. Many of the features were common in other grand Elizabethan houses.

The layout of houses like Hardwick Hall reflected a change in how society worked. Unlike in the medieval period, country houses were no longer the centre of village life. Instead they were designed for the comfort of their owners and their guests. An increased number of rooms allowed greater privacy and the separation of servants into their own quarters reflects the strict social structure of Elizabethan society.

The medieval great hall was replaced by the great chamber, a place to welcome guests. At Hardwick Hall, the high great chamber was elaborately decorated to demonstrate both taste and wealth. In the long gallery, another common part of Elizabethan houses, portraits and other features depicted family connections, as it was important to show that social status went back over many generations, rather than being gained through recent wealth. At Hardwick, a carved overmantel depicts figures from the Hardwick family and from the family of Bess's second husband, Sir William Cavendish, whose social position had been higher for much longer than Bess's family. With similar aims, the stonework on the front of the house included the carved letters 'ES' – Elizabeth Shrewsbury – along with the Hardwick coat of arms. These were important ways of showing the wealth and status of the family.

EXAMINER TIP

This is a clear and concise introduction that addresses the question.

EXAMINER TIP

This point is not developed. Much more could be said about how Elizabethan houses were different from what had gone before. The point about the strict structure of Elizabethan society could also be expanded.

EXAMINER TIP

This is a good link back to the question.

As well as displaying their wealth, Elizabethans also wanted to show how cultured they were. The height of fashion was the Italian Renaissance style. The stonework on Hardwick Hall reflects this as it follows an Italian design. Similarly, the loggia, or open walkway, also reflects the latest trends in Italian architecture. Inside, elaborate plasterwork reflected the latest fashions among Italian nobility. The emphasis on perfect design is clear at Hardwick with the decision to place the straight chimney columns within internal walls so that the house would remain symmetrical.

A final way of showing wealth for Elizabethan nobles was through the use of expensive materials like glass. The more glass a building contained, the richer the owner usually was. It was not possible to make large pieces of glass and so small pieces were placed within lattice frames. The technology needed to do this was expensive and the amount of glass featured in Hardwick Hall was a deliberate effort to show the wealth of its owner. Descriptions from the time describe the house as being 'more window than wall'.

Hardwick Hall strongly supports the statement that Elizabethan stately homes were a way of showing the wealth and status of their owners. Like many other grand houses of the period, every element of the design was included for this purpose. People like Bess of Hardwick wished to demonstrate their wealth through the size of the building and features like the huge windows; they wanted to show their status through their decoration both inside and out and to demonstrate their cultured tastes through the use of elaborate Italian design. Hardwick Hall clearly reflects this.

EXAMINER TIP

Ensure all points are relevant to the question and that your answer does not become simply a description of the building or location of the historic environment.

OVERALL COMMENT

This is a Level 3 answer. It demonstrates a good knowledge of Hardwick Hall and places it in the context of Elizabethan houses more generally. It could be improved by showing wider knowledge and understanding of other reasons why homes like Hardwick Hall were built.

OVER TO YOU

1 What are the strengths of this answer? Reread it and then use a highlighter to identify its good elements.

2 What could be improved? Can you make any additions to the answer that would improve its quality?

3 Have a go at writing your own answer to the question (allow yourself a maximum of 20 minutes). Once you have written an answer, ask yourself the following:

   a Have you shown a good knowledge of the site, why it was built in the location and form that it was?

   b Have you explained what it tells you about the period, linking it to your wider historical knowledge?

   c Have you come to a clear conclusion that answers the question?

REVIEW

Look back at pages 22–23 on wealth in Elizabethan England. This will help you to make suggestions on how to improve this answer.

The answers provided here are examples, based on the information provided in the Recap sections of this Revision Guide. There may be other factors which are relevant to each question, and you should draw on as much of your own knowledge as possible to give detailed and precise answers. There are also many ways of answering exam questions (for example, of structuring an essay). However, these exemplar answers should provide a good starting point.

Chapter 1 Page 13
EXPLAIN

a They may be trusted by the queen or they might be a powerful landowner.

b The Privy Council was responsible for the day-to-day running of the country and for advising the queen.

WRITE AN ACCOUNT

Answer might include:

- A description of the parts of Elizabethan government (Privy Council, Parliament, Lord Lieutenants and Justices of the Peace).
- An explanation of the roles of these parts e.g. the Privy Council took responsibility for the day-to-day running of the country and the Lord Lieutenants took responsibility for a particular part of the country.

Chapter 2 Page 15
EXPLAIN

a Answer might include:

- Succession: concerns over instability of the monarchy; the possibility of a Catholic queen.
- Religion: threat of Catholic rebellion (including Mary, Queen of Scots as an alternative queen).
- Puritanism: a threat to the religious settlement, many Puritans wanted to make the Church of England more extreme.
- Foreign policy: the threat of invasion; the opposition of the Pope to Elizabeth's rule.
- Taxation: unpopular taxes could lead to opposition.
- Ireland: instability could lead to the

loss of Ireland, which would lead to Elizabeth appearing weak. Ireland posed the threat of revolt and then the invasion of England.

- Mary, Queen of Scots: at the beginning of Elizabeth's reign, Mary, Queen of Scots, is married to the King of France. If Elizabeth died childless, then Mary, Queen of Scots, would be next in line to the throne and England might come under the control of France.

b Answer might include:

- A summary of the key problems.
- An explanation as to why the problems were important at the beginning of Elizabeth's reign; for example, religious problems could bring instability – she needed a new religious settlement. Mary, Queen of Scots, was also a potential threat at the beginning of Elizabeth's reign. Since Elizabeth was childless, a disputed succession could cause civil war.

Page 17
EXPLAIN

a Answer might include:

- To make or cement a foreign alliance.
- To guarantee loyalty from an English family.
- To produce an heir to stop a Catholic succeeding her to the throne.

b Answer is likely to include three of the following:

- The possibility of marriage helped Elizabeth to maintain loyalty from powerful men in England.
- Marriage could be used as a bargaining tool when dealing with foreign leaders.
- It avoided her authority being challenged by her husband.
- It maintained England's independence.
- It allowed her to dedicate her life to England.

c This is likely to include points from the two answers above, but might also include reference to her experiences as a child. For example, you might say

that the lack of an heir was a concern to England's Protestants as it meant that should Elizabeth die, the Catholic Mary, Queen of Scots, would come to the throne.

INTERPRETATION ANALYSIS

b Elizabeth did not marry because of her experiences as a child.

c Answer might include:

- It is convincing because it gives a clear explanation about why Elizabeth did not marry. Own knowledge might include:
  - That Dudley and Elizabeth were widely believed to have been in love.
  - Dudley's wife's death was seen as a convenient (and suspicious) event which allowed him to become available to marry the Queen.
- It is less convincing because Elizabeth would have also witnessed other marriages while growing up and she came close to marrying on a number of occasions.
- It might include reference to specific suitors whom Elizabeth nearly married.

Page 19
EXPLAIN

a **Difficulties between Elizabeth and Parliament**: Issues over marriage, free speech and monopolies. Religious difference.

Examples of when the relationship was good: Agreements over monopolies and poor laws. There was also some agreement on religious points and foreign affairs.

b Answer might include:

- It limited Elizabeth's power and affected her policies.
- It represented the wealth of the country. Its opinions mattered to reflect those of the Shires.

a Answer might include:

- advising Elizabeth.
- passing laws.
- setting taxes.

b You should produce your own poster.

c Answer must demonstrate a knowledge of Elizabeth's relationship with Parliament and the tensions that arose. Answer might include references to:

- Tensions over religion, free speech, marriage, monopolies.
- Successes for Parliament – Mary, Queen of Scots, the Poor Law.
- Successes for Elizabeth – freedom of speech, monopolies, marriage, religion.

Page 21

EXPLAIN

a You should produce your own revision cards.

b The order will be your own.

WRITE AN ACCOUNT

a The spider diagram should include:

- Argument with Elizabeth at the Privy Council meeting.
- Failure in Ireland.
- Catching the queen without her wig.
- Loss of the monopoly/wealth and power.

b The flow chart needs to include all of the events listed in the 'Rebellion' box in the storyboard.

c Answer must include the causes, events and consequences of the rebellion. It needs to comment on the significance of the rebellion and its failure – and what this tells us about Elizabeth's authority at this point in her reign.

Chapter 3 Page 23

EXPLAIN

a Details might include:

- Nobility: most powerful; landowners; key members of Elizabeth's court; average income of £6000 a year; born into the position or (very

rarely) appointed to it by the queen; special privileges, such as protection from torture.
- Gentry: landowners; lived on the rents of their tenants; income varied between £10 and £200 a year; many served as Justices of the Peace or Members of Parliament; some given title of knight or esquire.
- Peasantry: worked as farm labourers; rising population and agricultural failures made work scarce and many lived in poverty.

b Answer might include:

- It was reflected in the structure of the society – the nobles, the gentry and the peasants.
- It reflected the superior position of the queen.
- It showed the importance of God in Elizabethan society.
- All the elements of the 'Great Chain' are linked together and have to stay together for the good order and functioning of society.

HISTORIC ENVIRONMENT

a The table is likely to include:

- Italian design, e.g. loggia – shows culture.
- Family portraits and decoration – show standing of family.
- Portraits of Elizabeth – show loyalty.
- Number of rooms – shows that privacy was more of a concern than during the medieval period.
- Rooms for entertaining – important part of wealthy Elizabethans' lives.

b Answer needs to include reference to both Hardwick Hall and wider contextual knowledge. They may include any of the following:

- The design of the house shows that security is no longer the priority.
- The inclusion of Italian styles, such as the loggia, reflects the height of Elizabethan fashion and demonstrates Bess's awareness of culture.
- The amount of glass used is a way of displaying wealth – glass was expensive.

- The layout of the house – great chamber and long gallery – shows the importance of entertaining.
- Artwork showing family members and ancestors was a way of showing social position – the overmantel in the long gallery.

Page 25

EXPLAIN

a Answer might include:

- Previously, different entertainment for the rich and the poor. Theatre was for the poor.
- Traditional plays had been performed by small troupes in inns and pubs. Now more new plays were written and performed.
- Elizabethan era saw patronage from nobles.
- Permanent theatres, such as the Globe.
- The rich and the poor watched the same performances.

b Answer might include:

- Change in how theatre worked and how people watched it.
- Showed the structure of society and could make political messages.
- Reflected the desire of the wealthy to seem cultured and fashionable – theatre became much more respectable.

HISTORIC ENVIRONMENT

a The spider diagram will include features shown in the illustration, including the parts of the stage and the audience positions.

b Answer might include:

- Reflects the structure of society – poor in the pit, gentry in the 'Gentlemen's rooms' and the nobility in the 'Lords' rooms' higher up.
- Elizabethan theatres were purpose-built so that different classes of people could come together in one location. In that sense they were designed to accommodate all classes sharing a common experience and by that fact the issues and values that are expressed/experienced through the play.

Page 27

a The table is likely to include the following, with some explanation:

Yes: art; exploration; theatre; buildings; literature; education; science and technology; peace; power; pride.

No: blood sports; torture and execution; divide between rich and poor; low life expectancy; poor medicine; questionable science (alchemy and astrology); the fact that it was a deliberate message spread by the government through Gloriana.

b The interpretation is saying that the Elizabethan era is remembered as a 'golden age' but recognises that there were also negative aspects to the period.

c Answer might include the following:

- It is convincing because it gives a number of reasons for the period being described as the 'Golden Age', such as exploration and the work of Shakespeare. People at the time recognised that there was something rather special about being alive at this Renaissance/ Elizabethan time.
- It also recognises the challenges of Elizabeth's reign such as war and religious conflict.
- It is less convincing in that it does not consider how the idea of the 'Golden Age' came about through Gloriana.

WRITE AN ACCOUNT

a The way in which Elizabeth and her government encouraged the idea of the 'Golden Age' through plays, festivals and pamphlets.

b Answer needs to weigh up the influence of Gloriana against the real accomplishments of the Elizabethan age. For example, the answer might argue that the idea of the 'Golden Age' was simply propaganda or that it genuinely was a time of great accomplishments.

Chapter 4 Page 29

EXPLAIN

a A pauper who is untrustworthy and has no interest in honest work. Examples include the Clapper Dudgeon and the Baretop Trickster.

b Make your own mind-map.

WRITE AN ACCOUNT

a Reasons could include: Henry VII's limit on private armies; closure of the monasteries (out of work monks and nuns plus lack of care for sick and old); failed harvests; enclosures; rising population; rack renting; inflation; flu outbreak of 1556.

b Answer might include any of the reasons listed above. There may also be links made between the reasons, for example, the failed harvests and rising population led to the increase in food prices and inflation.

Page 31

EXPLAIN

a Key differences are: Nationally the emphasis was on punishment. Many beggars were seen as undeserving and untrustworthy. It was up to individuals to help those genuinely in need through giving to charity. In the three cities listed, a more sympathetic approach was taken which encouraged and helped the poor to find work. The wealthy were expected to play their part through taxation.

b Answer might include:

- It was important because it showed a change in attitude toward how the poor should be dealt with.
- The schemes in London, York, Ipswich and Norwich acted as pilot schemes from which the 1601 Poor Law took inspiration and learned.

INTERPRETATION ANALYSIS

a Arguments for might include:

- It was a more sympathetic approach that focused on helping the vulnerable.
- Poverty was viewed less as a sin or crime that should be punished.
- It was acknowledged that some

people might be poor through no fault of their own.

Arguments against might include:

- Punishment was still a major part of how poverty was dealt with.
- It remained the responsibility of local authorities to deal with the poor.

b
- The interpretation suggests that although the 1601 law seemed to represent a change in attitude, in reality it did not. The poor remained the responsibility of local authorities and punishment was still seen as a reasonable way to deal with poverty. Answer should explain whether you agree with the author or not.

c Answer might include:
- It is convincing because it recognises the success of some towns and cities and that these ideas spread to the rest of the country.
- It is convincing because it accurately explains why the Poor Law was successful while also outlining its flaws.
- It is less convincing because it does not fully recognise the successes of the Poor Law – begging did decrease in England.

Chapter 5 Page 33

EXPLAIN

a New technology; improved defences; improved navigation.

b It allowed for safer and faster voyages, sailors were able to avoid dangerous waters and stay on (or get back on) course.

WRITE AN ACCOUNT

a He circumnavigated the globe.

b The flow chart must include all key points of Drake's journey shown on the map.

c Answer likely to include: a detailed account of Drake's story, beginning with him setting sail from England. It is likely to make reference to the attempted mutiny; various problems with storms; raids on Spanish ports; and the claiming of 'New Albion'.

Page 35

a Answers might include: wealth (trade, raiding of Spanish ships and ports), territory (building new colonies), power (establishing dominance of the seas).

b The interpretation suggests that increasing wealth through trade was the main purpose of exploration.

c • Answer might include:
   o It is convincing because it talks about the establishment of spice routes and other trading routes. It explains why these were an important way of bringing wealth to England. The source also mentions patriotism: depriving enemy countries (i.e. Spain) of resources (i.e. gold and silver) could also be seen as fulfilling a patriotic duty.
   o It is less convincing because it does not consider the importance of building colonies or increasing English dominance of the seas, both of which were major reasons for exploration.
  • Answer must include contextual knowledge.

EXPLAIN

a The mind-map will include factors shown in the boxes on the spread.

b Answer might include:
  • Wealth through trade and raiding of Spanish ships and ports.
  • The establishment of colonies.
  • Increased dominance of England on the sea.

Chapter 6 Page 37

EXPLAIN

a One of the following: God created the world; Jesus was God's son; those who challenge the true faith must be punished.

b Catholic view/Protestant view: Pope is head of the Church/monarch is head of the Church; Bible and services in Latin/English; priests cannot/can marry; decorated churches/plain churches; priests are the link to God/prayer allows personal connection with God; transubstantiation/bread and wine *represents* body and blood.

---

c Answer might include:
  • It was important because it brought stability after the religious changes of the earlier Tudors, preventing civil war.
  • It was important because it led to rebellions.
  • It was important because it eventually led to conflict with the Pope and the rest of Catholic Europe.

WRITE AN ACCOUNT

a Storyboard must include details of the Northern Rebellion, the papal bull and the Ridolfi Plot.

b Answer might include: challenges from within England – the Northern Rebellion; the papal bull and challenges inspired by the Pope's opposition.

Page 39

EXPLAIN

a Throckmorton Plot; Babington Plot; Cardinal Allen and his seminary; the Jesuits.

b Outline your opinion and give reasons for it.

INTERPRETATION ANALYSIS

a A Catholic organisation whose aim was to convert Protestants back to Catholicism.

b The interpretation suggests that the Jesuits were not a threat to Elizabeth.

c Answer might include:
  • It is convincing because the Jesuits' aim was to convert people to Catholicism, not to overthrow the government or inspire rebellion.
  • It is less convincing because the Jesuits were Catholics and therefore followed the Pope. The Pope had made it clear to all Catholics that they should challenge Elizabeth's rule.
  • It is also less convincing because the Jesuits' presence in England was a threat to the stability of the religious settlement. They had come with the materials to spread their message and wished to engage in public debate.

Page 41

EXPLAIN

a Summary is likely to include: he was a Jesuit missionary to England; his aim was to convert English people to Catholicism; he travelled across the country making speeches; he was arrested, tortured and executed.

b Answer is likely to include: the belief that missionaries were a threat to peace and stability; the work of Campion and Parsons; the wider role of Jesuits and seminary priests.

WRITE AN ACCOUNT

a Flashcards must include all the laws listed in the table on the page.

b Contextual knowledge might include a reference to the threat from overseas, from Catholics in the North, from the Jesuit missionaries and recent plots against Elizabeth.

c Answer might include: the suggestion that Elizabeth became harsher in her treatment of Catholics; a summary of the laws that were passed; an account of the fate of Campion and others. It might also include the reasons for the change in policy: the threat from overseas, from Catholics in the North, from the Jesuit missionaries and recent plots against Elizabeth.

Page 43

WRITE AN ACCOUNT

a The spider diagram will be based on information in the text.

b • Presbyterian: a Protestant Church that believes bishops should be replaced by elders.
  • Prophesyings: meeting of Protestant clergy which usually involved criticising the Church of England. These meetings were led by Puritans.
  • Separatist: someone who wants to break away from the mainstream.

c Answer might include the key developments in hard-line Puritanism and separatist movements.

a He was a sympathiser and allowed prophesyings to go ahead.

b Whitgift was much stricter – he passed laws banning many puritan practices.

c Answer might include: he introduced laws that cracked down on Puritanism. This included a ban on unlicensed preaching and fines for not attending church.

Page 45

WRITE AN ACCOUNT

a Religion; power and influence.

b The table will include Northern, Ridolfi, Throckmorton, Babington and Essex.

c Answer might include: Elizabeth's changing approach – tolerance followed by increasingly harsh laws and then arrests and executions.

EXPLAIN

a Cards will include: spies; unconvincing alternatives; punishments; religious settlement; a skilled politician.

b The order will depend on personal thoughts and opinions.

c Answers might include her network of spies, which made plotting against her incredibly difficult, and her popularity, which meant that most would not join a rebellion.

Chapter 7 Page 47

EXPLAIN

a The flow chart should use the key events outlined in the first section of the text.

b She was a Catholic and the heir to the English throne. Many Protestants felt that she might lead or inspire a rebellion. Even if she did not do this, she was still on course to become queen when Elizabeth died. Protestants feared a return to the horrors of Mary I's reign.

WRITE AN ACCOUNT

a Answer must include:
  • Catholic plot.
  • Led by Anthony Babington.
  • Planned to kill Elizabeth and place Mary on the throne.
  • Babington sent a coded message to Mary and she replied giving her support.
  • The servants were working for Walsingham and so the plot was uncovered.

b Answer might include:
  • It was the first evidence of direct involvement of Mary in a plot against Elizabeth.
  • It showed Elizabeth just how dangerous Mary could be. There was real evidence that Mary had committed treason in this plot.
  • It left Elizabeth little choice but to put Mary on trial and execute her.

Page 49

INTERPRETATION ANALYSIS

a • Mary's arrival caused problems because she was a Catholic queen and therefore someone for Catholic opponents of Elizabeth to see as an alternative monarch.
  • Walsingham provided evidence that Mary supported the Babington Plot, in form of coded messages.
  • Elizabeth was concerned that by killing a queen, she has created a martyr and established the idea that executing queens was acceptable. In some ways she had increased the Catholic threat.

b Answer is likely to include: It is convincing because it shows how Elizabeth struggled in how to deal with Mary. It also shows that her spy master, Walsingham, saw her as a genuine threat.

EXPLAIN

a Storyboard will contain key events shown in this chapter.

b Answer might include:
  • Her death removed an alternative

monarch for Elizabeth's enemies.
  • The heir to the throne was no longer a Catholic. It made Mary's Protestant son, James VI of Scotland, Elizabeth's heir.
  • It established the idea that monarchs could be executed for treason.

Chapter 8 Page 51

EXPLAIN

a Revision cards should include: marriage; papal bull; Catholicism versus Protestantism; sailors' actions; the Netherlands.

b Order depends on personal opinion.

c Answer might include:
  • The conflict increased religious tensions between Catholics and Protestants.
  • England's interference angered Philip.
  • The arrival of troops in 1584 was seen as an act of war.
  • With William of Orange dead Elizabeth was the most important Protestant ruler in Europe.

WRITE AN ACCOUNT

a Turning points might include: the death of Mary I; the papal bull; the actions of Sir Francis Drake and other English sailors, e.g. the 'singeing of the King of Spain's beard'; the assassination of William of Orange by a Spanish Catholic; Elizabeth's decision to send English troops to the Netherlands.

b Answer might include:
  • The lack of marriage between Philip and Elizabeth.
  • Raids of Spanish ships and ports by English sailors.
  • Conflict in the Netherlands.
  • The papal bull of 1570.
  • Religious difference.
  • The arrival of Jesuit and seminary priests from 1580 onwards.

Page 53

EXPLAIN

a The mind-map should include: tactics, size of fleet and new technology.

b Answer needs to explain reasons for choice.

c Answer might include:

- Better navigation allowed sailors to find their position more easily and to travel safely through hostile waters.
- Lateen sails allowed for faster travel to battle or through hostile waters.
- More powerful cannons meant that it was now possible to fire on enemy ships from a distance.
- More manoeuvrable ships made battle easier.

WRITE AN ACCOUNT

a John Hawkins.

b New technologies were developed; the size of the navy increased; new tactics were employed.

Page 55

WRITE AN ACCOUNT

a Timeline should include all dates shown on the map.

b Answer is likely to include the context of the Armada and the reasons for its failure outlined in the spider diagram.

HISTORIC ENVIRONMENT

a Answer needs to include specific detail about the role played by English tactics, Spanish mistakes and the weather.

b Answer needs to be fully explained.

c Answer might include:

- Tactics like fireships played a major role in the Spanish Armada and other sea battles.

- Improved weapons gave the English the advantage against the Armada because the Spanish did not have the correct weapons.
- Leaders like Drake were experienced and skilled tacticians.
- Poor planning could be disastrous, as it was with the Spanish Armada.
- The weather often played a key role – for example, in the Spanish Armada, the weather destroyed many ships. Although by this point the Armada had already been defeated.

almshouse charity building set up to provide food and rest for the poor

astrolabe a navigation tool that allowed for much more accuracy at sea

circumnavigate to travel all the way around something

colony land controlled by another country

Counter-Reformation the reform of the Catholic Church in Rome in the sixteenth and seventeenth centuries, in response to the Protestant Reformation

enclosure an area surrounded by a barrier

excommunicate officially remove from the Catholic Church by order of the Pope

exile being sent to live in another country that is not your own, especially for political reasons

fireship a burning ship sent into an enemy convoy or harbour

House of Correction where beggars would be forced to spend the night as punishment

inflation a currency becoming worth less, shown through rapidly rising prices

Jesuit a group within Catholicism whose aim is to spread the religion

lateen a triangular sail that was invented in the sixteenth century; it allowed ships to move much more quickly

line of battle a naval tactic used in battle; ships line up to create a long wall of cannon fire

martyr someone who has died for their religious beliefs

missionary someone whose aim is to spread their religious faith

monopoly the exclusive right to trade in a particular product

papal bull special message issued by the Pope

patron someone who funds the work of an artist or performing group

patronage land, titles or power given to ensure an individual's support

pauper the poorest members of society who were unable to find work

Pope the head of the Catholic Church

Presbyterian a Protestant Church that believes bishops should be replaced by elders

privateer a ship's captain with royal permission to attack foreign ships

Privy Council a monarch's private counsellors

prophesying a meeting of Protestant clergy which usually involved criticism of the English Church under Elizabeth

rack renting demanding an excessive or extortionate rent from a tenant or for a property

recusancy when a person refused to attend services of the Church of England

Renaissance the revival of European art and literature under the influence of classical civilisations in the fourteenth to sixteenth centuries

royal court the nobles, advisors and others who surrounded the monarch

Secretary of State the leader of the Privy Council; a very powerful position

seminary a training college for priests

separatist someone who wants to break away from the mainstream

stocks method of punishment for begging and other crimes; criminals would be held by the hands and feet while people threw things at them

succeed to take over the throne

surplice a white gown worn by priests in the Church of England

Notes

Notes

Notes

Topics available from *Oxford AQA GCSE History*

Student Books and Kerboodle Books

Paper One: understanding the modern world

Period Study

Germany 1890–1945 Democracy and Dictatorship
Student Book
978 019 837010 9
Kerboodle Book
978 019 837014 7

America 1920–1973 Opportunity and Inequality
Student Book
978 019 841262 5
Kerboodle Book
978 019 841263 2

Wider World Depth Study

Conflict and Tension: The Inter-War Years 1918–1939
Student Book
978 0 19 837011 6
Kerboodle Book
978 019 837015 4

Conflict and Tension between East and West 1945–1972
Student Book
978 019 841266 3
Kerboodle Book
978 019 841267 0

Conflict and Tension in Asia 1950–1975
Student Book
978 019 841264 9
Kerboodle Book
978 019 841265 6

Conflict and Tension: First World War 1894–1918
Student Book
978 019 842900 5
Kerboodle Book
978 019 842901 2

Paper Two: Shaping the nation

Thematic Study

Thematic Studies c790–Present Day
Student Book
978 019 837013 0
Kerboodle Book
978 019 837017 8

Contents include **all 3 Thematic Study options**: Health, Power, and Migration, Empires and the People

British Depth Study

British Depth Studies c1066–1685
Student Book
978 019 837012 3
Kerboodle Book
978 019 837016 1

Contents include **all 4 British Depth Study options**: Norman, Medieval, Elizabethan, and Restoration England

---

Covering all 16 options

Teacher Handbook

Teacher Handbook
978 019 837018 5

Kerboodle Exam Practice and Revision

Kerboodle Exam Practice and Revision
978 019 837019 2

Revision Guides (◉) RECAP (⚙) APPLY (↻) REVIEW (✓) SUCCEED

Germany 1890–1945 Democracy and Dictatorship
Revision Guide: 978 019 842289 1
Kindle edition: 978 019 842290 7

America 1920–1973 Opportunity and Inequality
Revision Guide: 978 019 843282 1
Kindle edition: 978 019 843283 8

Conflict and Tension: The Inter-War Years 1918–1939
Revision Guide: 978 019 842291 4
Kindle edition: 978 019 842292 1

Conflict and Tension between East and West 1945–1972
Revision Guide: 978 019 843288 3
Kindle edition: 978 019 843289 0

Conflict and Tension in Asia 1950–1975
Revision Guide: 978 019 843286 9
Kindle edition: 978 019 843287 6

Britain: Power and the People c1170–Present Day
Revision Guide: 978 019 843290 6
Kindle edition: 978 019 843291 3

Health and the People c1000–Present Day
Revision Guide: 978 019 842295 2
Kindle edition: 978 019 842296 9

Norman England c1066–c1100
Revision Guide: 978 019 843284 5
Kindle edition: 978 019 843285 2

Elizabethan England c1568–1603
Revision Guide: 978 019 842293 8
Kindle edition: 978 019 842294 5

Order online at **www.oxfordsecondary.co.uk/aqa-gcse-history**

OXFORD